I0889580

Phantoms of Christmas Past

Festive Ghost Hoaxes, Ghost Hunts and Ghost Panics

What People Are Saying About

Phantoms of Christmas Past

A superb collection of festive ghost tales! A must-read for those who enjoy a traditional Christmas ghost story or for those who enjoy paranormal accounts.
GL Davies, author of *Haunted: Horror of Haverfordwest*

An extraordinary potpourri of ghostly hoaxes and panics which are sure to entertain, surprise and spook.
Dr John Jacob Woolf, author of *The Wonders: Lifting the Curtain on the Freak Show, Circus and Victorian Age*

True tales of fake ghosts, along with their motives and consequences. Essential reading for historians, psychologists, folklorists and ghost hunters.
Andy Owens, paranormal author and blogger

With Weatherhead's ghosts, you can generally see right through them ... His collection of transparent tales offers a refreshing take on a familiar – but still happily weird – genre.
John Billingsley, author, historian, and folklorist

Phantoms of Christmas Past

Festive Ghost Hoaxes, Ghost Hunts, and Ghost Panics

Paul Weatherhead

6TH
BOOKS

London, UK
Washington, DC, USA

CollectiveInk

First published by Sixth Books, 2025
Sixth Books is an imprint of Collective Ink Ltd.,
Unit 11, Shepperton House, 89 Shepperton Road, London, N1 3DF
office@collectiveinkbooks.com
www.collectiveinkbooks.com
www.6th-books.com

For distributor details and how to order please visit the 'Ordering' section on our website.

Text copyright: Paul Weatherhead 2024

ISBN: 978 1 80341 840 7
978 1 80341 866 7 (ebook)
Library of Congress Control Number: 2024936885

All rights reserved. Reproduction or translation of any part of this book through any means without permission of the copyright owner is unlawful, except for promotional use. Request for other permissions or further information should be addressed in writing to the author.

The rights of Paul Weatherhead as author have been asserted in accordance with the Copyright, Designs and Patents Act 1988.

A CIP catalogue record for this book is available from the British Library.

Design: Lapiz Digital Services

UK: Printed and bound by CPI Group (UK) Ltd, Croydon, CR0 4YY
Printed in North America by CPI GPS partners

This book is not intended as a substitute for professional medical advice. The reader should consult the appropriate healthcare professional regarding specific needs. All client names used herein are pseudonyms to protect privacy.

We operate a distinctive and ethical publishing philosophy in all areas of our business, from our global network of authors to production and worldwide distribution.

I don't believe in ghosts. I've seen far too many myself!

Samuel Taylor Coleridge

Contents

Introduction

The bleak midwinter is a border between the old year and the new, and borders have always had a mysterious, exotic, or magical quality. Whether it's the border between land and sea, sleeping and waking, or life and death, this is where one world meets another. Folklorists use the word 'liminal' to denote this threshold, and many of the true stories in this book have a liminal quality. This is because they exist in the border between reality and imagination, tradition and progress, village and city, truth and delusion, life and death, the past and the present. It's these liminal spaces that are haunted by the phantoms in this book.

These are true stories of Christmas and New Year phantoms from the nineteenth and early twentieth centuries. The word phantom was chosen deliberately for its ambiguity. On the one hand, it's a synonym for ghost, but it also has the further meaning of something that is an illusion. This book isn't about whether ghosts exist or not. It's about what happens when ghostly legends, ghost hunters, and ghost hoaxers collide. The results are sometimes tragic, sometimes comic, sometimes scary, and often bizarre.

Ghost Hoaxes

The ghost hoaxes in this book generally fall into three categories: playing the ghost, poltergeist jinx, and journalistic jokes. The first of these, playing the ghost, is the deliberate act of dressing up in a ghostly costume and scaring people in a public place. This might sound like an odd thing to do, but the activity was rife throughout the nineteenth and early twentieth centuries, and could cause considerable disruption, disorder, fear, and panic in the community. At its simplest, a man (it almost invariably was a man) would don a white sheet or tablecloth and prance around in a moonlit graveyard or other atmospheric location, often causing a local sensation. Should anyone give chase, he could whip the sheet off and vanish into the darkness. Some costumes, as we shall see in this book, were more inventive and elaborate. The Hammersmith Monster of 1824 (chapter two), for example, was said to breathe fire and have metallic claws attached to his hands. The Lochee Ghost (chapter five) that prowled the street of west Dundee in the winter of 1900 had an unearthly luminous hat. These 'ghosts' were frequently reported to jump out on lone women, often shocking them into fits.

The second category of ghost hoax is poltergeist jinx. The word poltergeist originates from the German words for 'noisy ghost', and as such poltergeists tend to be heard and not seen. However, poltergeist phenomena are some of the easiest to hoax simply by throwing things when nobody is looking, using threads to pull ornaments off shelves and other ingenious methods which we will encounter presently. Outbreaks of supposed poltergeist activity were frequently reported in the press in the nineteenth and early twentieth centuries and generated a lot of interest. As we shall see, sometimes these episodes generated too much interest, as in the cases of the Peterborough Poltergeist (chapter three) and the Violet Farm Poltergeist (chapter six) where ghost hunters were almost as much of a nuisance as the supposed hauntings themselves.

The third category is the journalistic joke. It was quite common for newspapers to invent comic ghost stories, especially at Christmas, to fill a few column inches and sell a few extra papers. So much the better if the newspaper's rivals took the story seriously and reprinted it, as in the case of the Ghost of King Richard III on New Year's Eve in 1921 (chapter nine).

Ghost Hunts

Where there are reports of ghosts, you also find various ghost hunters, and these feature throughout the stories in this book. The most respectable of these investigators were from the Society for Psychical Research (SPR), established in 1882 to further the scientific study of supposedly supernatural phenomena.[1] The Society had many eminent scientists among its members, including Sir Oliver Lodge and Sir William Crooke as well as other luminaries such as psychologist William James and author Sir Arthur Conan Doyle. Conan Doyle was not happy with the Society's sceptical approach and went on to lead a mass defection from the SPR after it had exposed the shenanigans of several fraudulent Spiritualist mediums. The Sherlock Holmes author was, of course, a Spiritualist himself, and it's no surprise that reports of ghostly activity attracted mediums and Spiritualists anxious to try and contact the restless spirit through seances. Spiritualism was huge in the nineteenth and early twentieth centuries, and friends in high places such as prominent newspaper editor W.T. Stead gave them sympathetic column inches. The rivalry between the SPR with its attempts at scientific rigour and the Spiritualist mediums (whose seances always seemed to pluck a ghost from the ether) is part of the background to our stories, and some of the august gentlemen mentioned above make brief appearances in the true stories collected here.

The SPR and the Spiritualists were not the only ones chasing ghosts. When the local community suspected a prankster was dressing as a ghost in order to scare people after dark, a very different ghost hunt was likely to ensue. These involved volunteer vigilantes that would roam the streets after dark hoping to catch the hoaxer in the act of playing the ghost. Some would be armed with sticks, clubs, or worse and anyone caught larking around with a sheet over his head was likely to receive little sympathy. It's fair to say that these unofficial patrols were probably not particularly sober – perhaps especially if it was Christmas – and would sometimes turn carnivalesque as the burly young men would dress up in women's clothes hoping to act as a honey trap for the ghost prankster. Although this sounds rather comic, and it surely was seen as a great laugh by the participants, these ghost hunts could also end in tragedy, as we shall see in the story of the Hammersmith Ghost in chapter one. We shall come across these ghost hunting vigilantes a number of times in the course of the book.

However, the most riotous ghost hunts were carried out by ghost flash mobs. When reports of ghost sightings appeared in newspapers, it was very common for people to gather at the scene of the haunting. Here they could exchange stories and rumours about the ghost, and perhaps even catch a glimpse of it. Crowds could grow to hundreds and even thousands, in which case police struggled to control the situation. These impromptu hunts could be drunken riots with friends jumping out on each other for a lark, wild goose chases in and among the gravestones, drunks screaming and shrieking as if they were ghosts, all the while canny pickpockets picked their way through the distracted crowds plying their trade. Christmas time would increase the merriment of these boisterous spontaneous parties, which in the strange story of the Clanking Ghost of East Barnet (chapter twelve) became an annual event every Christmas for years. Ghost flash mobs were common in the nineteenth and early twentieth century and are a fascinating piece of a forgotten history.

Ghost Panics

People don't have ideas. Ideas have people. Although this bon mot is usually attributed to psychologist Carl Jung, it's more likely to be folk wisdom, perhaps inspired by the psychologist. Nevertheless, there is truth in it – panic and hysteria can seize populations and blow through communities causing havoc and widespread fear. Rumours of ghosts sometimes caused these kinds of panics, and when this happened people would be afraid to go out at night, members of the community would eye each other with suspicion if their paths crossed after dark, each suspecting the other was a 'ghost' about to prank them. False alarms and wild goose chases would ensue and sometimes people (or the press) would make up or imagine ghostly encounters, all adding to the chaos. Throw in some sensational newspaper coverage and perhaps a reward offered for the capture of the 'ghost', some armed and angry vigilantes and you have a recipe for a ghost panic. Sometimes these ghost scares resemble what we might call phantom attacker panics, when a community under stress becomes convinced that an imaginary malevolent assailant is stalking their streets or meaning to do them harm.

A classic example of a phantom attacker panic is the case of the Halifax Slasher.[2] In the November of 1938, reports began to emerge of a razor blade wielding maniac roaming the streets of Halifax and mounting violent and terrifying slashing attacks on his mostly female victims. The fear of this attacker led to vigilante mobs roaming the streets, businesses staying closed, and widespread fear and panic. The attacks escalated beyond police control and then, strangely, the horrible assaults spread across the country. Finally, Scotland Yard arrived in Halifax and began to re-interview the victims. One by one, the victims (in Halifax and around the country) admitted they had slashed themselves and made up the story of the mystery attacker. It was a classic case of mass social panic, a kind of collective delusion. Something similar may be happening in some of the ghost panics we will examine in this book, for example in the case of the Lochee Ghost (chapter five) that sent the people of west Dundee into a frenzy over Christmas 1900.

Why Christmas?

The kinds of ghost hoaxes, hunts and panics related in this book happened all year round, though they frequently occurred over the Christmas and New Year period, and it is these I've selected for inclusion. There are several possibilities as to why these episodes so often happened at this time of year. Obviously, if one is going to dress as a ghost and scare people, darkness is an advantage that makes winter nights ideal. Longer hours of darkness may lead to an increase in nervousness and anxiety in people, making them more susceptible to fear, panic and hysteria. Lonely places like graveyards or empty streets look spooky on a winter's night, so this is understandable. Furthermore, would-be ghost hoaxers and vigilante ghost hunters may be more likely to fortify themselves with some Christmas spirit at the festive time of year, leading to more unrestrained and mischievous behaviour. However, it's also a distinct possibility that newspapers were simply more likely to devote space to such episodes around Christmas due to its traditional association with ghost stories.

The stories I've unearthed for this book all took place around Christmas and New Year between the early nineteenth and the early twentieth centuries. However, many of these ghost hunts, hoaxes and panics echo ghostly folklore or horrific events from previous centuries, as can be seen with the Calverley Ghost of Yorkshire and the horrendous murders associated with it (chapter eight), or the Lochee Ghost and the legend of the Indian Princess (chapter five). These episodes show what happens when legend, rumour, hoaxes, imagination, and particular social conditions combine.

In any case, I hope you enjoy these strange and mostly forgotten little episodes from history.

Wishing you a spooky Christmas and a scary New Year.

Author website: www.paulweatherhead.com

Chapter One

The Hammersmith Ghost

'Damn you, who are you? And what are you? Speak, or I'll shoot...'

(Francis Smith, 1804)

Some said the Hammersmith Ghost of the winter of 1803–04 was the spirit of a suicide victim who appeared as a sinister white figure with glowing eyes and who could sink into the earth without trace. Others said it had horns upon its head and breathed fire and smoke. However, many suspected a prankster was at work and although some brave souls gave chase to the Hammersmith Ghost, none could catch it. But when exciseman turned vigilante, Francis Smith decided to lie in wait for the spirit armed with a musket, there were tragic consequences...

The Suicide's Tale

Thomas Flynn was a dissolute and violent man. The Irishman, who worked as a clerk in a London cotton warehouse, was so cruel to his wife that in August 1800, complaining of ill-treatment, she left him and 'swore the peace' against him. This meant that she had a court order recognising her fear of physical violence from her husband, and furthermore that Flynn was forbidden from seeing her. Mrs Flynn moved in with her mother in Hammersmith, and Flynn fell into depressed spirits.

On Friday 8 August 1800 Flynn left his home in Brook Green and went to Hammersmith to see his wife, whom he believed was going to move in with another man. When Mrs Flynn answered the door, Flynn asked her to come back with him. She refused. He then asked if he could come in for a cup of tea, which she again refused. Finally, he asked if she would just shake his hand before he left. Again, she declined. Flynn said that if he could not have her then 'no other should' and grasping a poker plunged it into his wife's head before beating her violently with it and leaving her for dead.

Flynn ran to the Mall where he took a knife and cut his own throat and then stabbed himself in several places, aiming for his heart. He was taken to hospital where he spent some time walking up and down the wards in a state of delirium and writing letters before dying from his injuries in the early hours of Tuesday 12 August. His wife, though grievously injured, survived the attack.[1] Because Flynn had committed suicide, or 'self-murder' as it was generally referred to at the time, magistrates ordered that his body be buried under a crossroad. This caused outrage among the Irish community and crowds gathered around the hospital in which Flynn's body was being held. There was a fear that the body might be stolen to prevent such an ignominious and shameful burial. On the sixteenth of August soldiers had to be brought in to form a protective ring around the burial site, where three roads crossed at Hyde Park Corner.[2]

The burial of suicides under crossroads appears to have been standard practice from the late sixteenth century until the end of the eighteenth century. By 1800 there were around thirty reported suicides a year in London and digging up crossroads to bury them was causing too much disruption, so most bodies of people who had taken their own lives were given over to family to inter quietly.[3] Burial under a crossroad was now only reserved for cases where the authorities wished to set an example, and Thomas Flynn's was one of these. The practice was outlawed in 1823.

A number of explanations have been put forward to explain why suicides were buried under crossroads. One possibility is that crossroads symbolise the Christian cross, and this prevents the restless spirit from haunting the earth.[4] Another possibility is that the crossroads would confuse the ghost as it would not know which path to take to haunt the living.[5] Both of these explanations reflect the concern that, like the spirits of murderers, the spirits of suicides would likely be restless. The practice was perhaps also a kind of exorcism from the community, as if the suicide was a kind of vampire. Indeed, people who were buried at crossroads were often staked through the heart before being tumbled into the grave without a coffin and buried under cover of darkness.[6] It's not recorded whether Flynn's corpse was staked before he was dropped into his grave, but the controversy over his burial and the shock of his attempted murder of his wife would surely have been fresh in the minds of the people of Hammersmith, still a relatively small and rural community.

Crossroads are a liminal location, where worlds meet. In folklore they are associated with ghosts, witches, black magic rituals and, of course, are the place to go if one wants to sell one's soul to the devil. It's little wonder that when ghostly forms were seen around Hammersmith in the winter of 1803, the thoughts of many of Hammersmith's residents would turn to Thomas Flynn and the awful events of 1800. Had his restless spirit come back to haunt them?

The Hammersmith Ghost

At the start of the nineteenth century, Hammersmith was still an area of farms, plant nurseries and orchards, though it would soon be swallowed up by London, the fast-growing city it had been feeding.[7] But in October 1803, rumours of strange goings on began circulating among the locals and causing a great deal of unease. First, there were stories of what was assumed to be a mad woman wearing 'strange and uncouth dresses' cavorting in the churchyard at night and haunting the surrounding lanes. The unsettling behaviour of this woman and its nocturnal graveyard setting was disturbing to the locals, and no doubt stories and gossip as to who she was were exchanged. However, Mr Moody, the landlord of the Six Bells pub, had seen the figure and recognised the face – it belonged to a young lad, apprentice to a local butcher. The boy had been trying to scare, annoy or get the attention of a fellow servant by putting on her dresses and other clothes and frolicking in the churchyard and its surroundings. We are told the boy was reprimanded for his foolish behaviour and desisted from such escapades in the future.[8]

As winter drew in, other uncanny figures started to haunt Hammersmith. One ghostly apparition was draped in a white shroud, or perhaps, more likely a white sheet or tablecloth, but coming across it on a dark lane was certainly enough to give someone a fright. This 'ghost' was chased by angry locals a few times but was so fast and agile that he could escape his pursuers and vanish into the night.[9]

In one instance, chimney sweep, Mr Brazier, was walking home along Church Lane on a particularly dark night when he came face to face with a pale shrouded spectre in white. For a moment he froze at the sight, but then he held his walking stick out in front of him and approached the ghost, addressing it as he inched towards it: 'Ghost! Or whatever you may be, pray be civil.' However, when the chimney sweep got within touching distance, his stick did not pass through an ethereal or ghostly form. It prodded something much more solid – a young woman. Miss G_________, as she was named, had been having a lark with a male companion and dressing up as a ghost.[10]

As Christmas approached, the ghost (or ghosts) became more audacious. On 15 December, Thomas Groom, a brewer's servant was returning home with a friend at 10pm along a dark Hammersmith Lane when he encountered something strange. Unlike the previous ghostly sightings, this apparition was reported as being dressed in a calfskin with large horns and cloven feet. Groom, who was described as a 'stout and able man', was accosted by the uncanny figure and almost choked. Subsequent newspaper reports say that he was afterwards confined to his bed from the shock.[11] Strangely, other press accounts of the attack on Groom tell a slightly different story. According to the *Saint James's Chronicle,* the servant saw something white flitting between the tombs of the churchyard and then felt someone chuck him under the chin. He stretched out his hand and felt something soft rather like a sheet or tablecloth, but couldn't see anything. Soon afterwards Groom saw something white turn the corner and he and his companion chased it only for it to disappear into the darkness.[12]

Over the Christmas period, the beleaguered residents of Hammersmith were seeing all kinds of visions, at least according to later newspaper reports. At Christmas, a coach driver travelling along a dark lane heard an unusual rustling noise. There in the moonlight, he saw a strange figure in white gliding over the meadow. As the phantom approached, the driver could see that it had bladders attached to its shoulders, arms, body and head, and these bladders appeared to be filled with dried peas causing them to rattle. Inflated pig bladders filled with dried peas were a grisly but common toy at the time.[13] In any case the driver leapt down from his coach and ran into town and returned to the scene with some brave men to investigate, but all they found was that the horses had apparently been unharnessed by the figure and were grazing in the meadow.[14]

Women and children were too scared to go out alone for fear of encountering the Hammersmith Ghost. Most sightings were of a figure in white, though as we have seen, some described the ghost as having horns and dressed in a calf skin or covered in rattling bladders. Rumours also spread about the ghost having eyes that had the appearance of glow worms or that he could breathe out fire and smoke and sink down into the earth to vanish without a trace.[15] Even stranger, some said the ghost appeared as Napoleon or sometimes as a headless horse.[16] Many of the locals, though, assumed the ghost was the restless spirit of Thomas Flynn. Flynn's violent death by his own hand, his guilty conscience, and his lack of a Christian burial all made him a perfect candidate for the ghost. However, more sceptical Hammersmith residents believed that the 'ghosts' were hoaxers larking about and deliberately scaring people as a callous prank, though press reports pointed out the serious consequences this could lead to. Several women and children had apparently nearly lost their minds with terror after encountering the ghost, and a superstitious old lady had gone mad with fright never to recover.[17]

Worst of all, a pregnant woman was reportedly scared to death. She had been crossing through Hammersmith churchyard returning home at around 10pm when she saw a tall, white ghostly figure rise from the tombstones. The woman tried to run but the ghost was too swift, caught her and pressed her in its arms. The woman fainted and was found unconscious by some neighbours and taken to her bed where she died two days later.[18]

In the days between Christmas and New Year, the atmosphere in Hammersmith was increasingly febrile as the community was gripped by a hysterical ghost panic.

The Tale of the Shoemaker's Apprentice

Ghost sightings continued over the Christmas period of 1803 and beyond, yet no one was fast enough to catch the culprit who was adept at disappearing into dark country lanes and avoiding his pursuers. One of the most important sightings for later tragic events was that of the shoemaker's apprentice. The shoemaker was John Graham of Dorvell's Row, Hammersmith. The job of escorting his servant Sarah Francis home at night – and with the ghost at large, it was certainly felt necessary for a woman to have an escort after dark – usually fell to the one-armed postman who lodged with Graham. However, on

Thursday 29 December, the postman had retired to bed early, and the shoemaker's apprentice was tasked with walking the young woman to her house through the dark winter lanes. On his way back home after completing his duty, he came face to face with the ghost by the public water pump.

The boy was terrified out of his mind and fled across the road where he met watchman William Girdler doing his rounds on Beaver Street. The boy told the watchman that he had seen the ghost and, looking across the road, Girdler was shocked to see that the boy was telling the truth. The Hammersmith Ghost – or at least a man in a white sheet – was standing on the opposite side of the road. The watchman gave chase, but the figure whipped off the sheet or tablecloth, tucked it under his arm and vanished into the darkness. Despite searches and enquiries at the White Hart pub as to whether anyone had seen a suspicious person, Girdler could find nothing. No doubt the watchman took this opportunity to steady his nerves with a festive tipple. At the same time, the ghostly figure was seen by Mrs Steward and her servant from their nearby terrace, causing them much alarm.[19]

With many people scared to go out at night for fear of encountering the ghost, and with colourful rumours of Devil horns, fire breathing and glowing eyes spreading through the community, something had to be done. Nighttime patrols by various young men had failed to catch the ghost. Even watchman William Girdler, who was paid to protect the locals, had failed to apprehend the culprit. It's easy to see why some might want to take the law into their own hands.

The Killer's Tale

Watchman William Girdler certainly had a motive to catch the ghost to make up for it eluding him on 29 December. Strangely, John Graham (the master of the terrified apprentice who had alerted Girdler to the ghost) had jeered at the watchman a few days later when he passed him in the street. 'Were not you very much frightened the other night?' he taunted the watchman. Girdler replied that he wasn't afraid and that whoever the ghost was, he would go to hell.[20] Surely, Girder would have seen Graham's comment as suspicious. Could he be the ghost? But to be sure, Girder needed to catch the ghost red-handed. To do this, he agreed to work with Hammersmith exciseman, Francis Smith.[21]

Smith and Girdler met in the White Hart pub on the night of Tuesday 3 January to make plans. They would go to Black Lion Lane, where the ghost had made his escape a number of times, and Smith would lie in wait, armed with a musket loaded with powder and a ball. Girdler would do his rounds keeping a lookout for the ghost, and if their paths crossed, they had decided on a password between them. One would say 'Friend! Who comes there?' and the other was to reply 'Advance friend'.[22]

The two men fortified themselves with some New Year spirit before setting out in search of the ghost. With Girdler on his rounds, Francis Smith, loaded gun in hand, settled in to wait for the appearance of the ghost in a state of some trepidation. It was a very dark night and a very dark lane. Close to midnight, Smith saw a figure in white emerging from the gloom. He challenged it but received no answer. Again, he shouted to the figure 'Damn you, who are you? And what are you? Speak, or I'll shoot.' When no reply came, and the white figure continued to approach, Smith took aim with his musket and fired.[23]

The Bricklayer's Tale

On the evening of 3 January, the last day of his life, Thomas Millwood (22) was dozing in front of the fire at his father's home where he lived. He was a bricklayer and plasterer and was still dressed in his work clothes – a white shirt, white flannel jacket and white trousers, the traditional dress for those in his profession. Millwood was woken by his sister

Anne around 10pm and told to go and meet his wife and escort her home. He took some persuading but, because it was a dark night and his pregnant wife would be walking home alone, he relented.[24] Perhaps the strange stories and rumours of ghostly antics in the lanes of Hammersmith played a role in Millwood's decision.

In any case, in his all-white working clothes, Millwood set off down the dark Hammersmith Lane. This was against the advice of his mother-in-law Phebe Colbrooke, who had warned him to wear a coat over his work clothes in case someone should mistake him for the Hammersmith Ghost. This had indeed happened on one occasion. Two ladies and a gentleman had been frightened after passing him on the street after dark. One of them had cried, 'There is the Ghost,' to which Millwood had replied testily that he was no more a ghost than they were and asked if they wanted a punch in the head.[25]

Francis Smith confronts the 'Ghost' as illustrated in the *Newgate Calendar* 1841

After her brother had left, Anne had a strange presentiment that something terrible was going to happen to him. She went outside the front door and stood on a pile of bricks and peered into the gloom but could not see him. She did, however, hear a voice cry: 'Damn you, who are you? And what are you? Speak, or I'll shoot.' Then she saw a bright flash followed by the sound of a gun firing. She ran inside and woke her parents, telling them she was sure that Thomas had been shot, but they told her that was impossible. Still feeling that a catastrophe had befallen her brother, she set out on her own along the lane that Thomas had taken and thirty yards from her home, saw a figure lying on his back with his arms stretched out at the crossroads where Beaver Lane met Black Lion Lane. She called out 'Brother!' and stooped to look at him. His face was bloody and burnt black with gunpowder. The musket ball had smashed through his left jaw and 'perforated every part of his head.' Anne ran screaming to a nearby house and the police were called.[26]

The watchman William Girdler had also heard the gunshot but had decided to ignore it and head to the pub. Gunshots were fairly common and he didn't give it much thought until a young woman accosted him and said he was needed. As Girdler headed in the direction of the gunshot, he met Francis Smith who said that he had shot the ghost. Smith didn't seem aware of the enormity of his actions until Girdler explained the situation he was in. Girdler told Smith to go home where he later surrendered himself to the police. Millwood's body was removed to the Black Lion pub to await the inquest. News of poor Millwood's death caused uproar in Hammersmith and over the next few days crowds of people pushed and jostled into the Black Lion pub hoping to catch a glimpse of the body.[27]

Thomas Millwood was buried on 8 January 1804 in the grounds of Hammersmith Chapel. The throng of people from far and near was so great that not even half of them could cram into the chapel for the service. The subject of the Hammersmith

Ghost was on everyone's lips as they shared stories, rumours, and gossip about the events of the last few weeks and gave their considered opinions as to the existence or non-existence of ghosts.

Millwood's widow had recently lost a child and was due to give birth to another in a few months.[28]

The Shoemaker's Tale

While Francis Smith languished in Newgate prison awaiting his trial for the murder of Thomas Millwood, a man he mistakenly thought was the Hammersmith Ghost, it was widely reported that the *real* Hammersmith Ghost had been caught. The ghost was named as shoemaker John Graham.[29] No doubt watchman William Girdler had suspected this on hearing Graham's barbed jibe at him after Graham's young apprentice had been scared by a figure in white back on 29 December of the previous year.

John Graham was described as a God-fearing man of good character who was married, with three children. He claimed he had impersonated a ghost in order to teach his young apprentice a lesson. The lad had been scaring Graham's children by filling their heads with ghost stories and making scratching noises on the walls so the children would think their house was haunted. On 29 December, the perfect opportunity arose for Graham to put his plan into action. The one-armed postman who normally escorted servant Sarah Francis home had gone to bed. Graham instructed his apprentice to see the girl home, and then he took his white sheet and waited by the public water pump for the boy to return.[30]

Graham's plan was highly effective. He certainly succeeded in terrifying his apprentice and then leading Hammersmith's bumbling watchman on a wild goose chase as well as being seen by several other witnesses. However, the press suggested that it was Graham's prank which inadvertently led to Francis Smith's vigilante ghost hunt, which of course led to the needless death of Thomas Millwood. It was also rather unfairly assumed that

Graham had been responsible for all the ghost hoaxing that had happened over the Christmas and New Year period.[31] Graham himself told the press that he had only donned the white sheet once, and that he was not the culprit behind other scares. Early reports said that Graham was brought before a magistrate, though it seems this was untrue. His prank may have been ill-timed, but it's unclear what crime he had committed.

In any case, there was surely public ill-feeling against Graham who seems to have become something of a scapegoat. A rumour spread that Graham was to be publicly shamed and forced to stand in the church wrapped in his white sheet for all to stare at. Vast numbers gathered to witness the spectacle, though of course it never happened.[32]

The Hammersmith Ghost pictured in *Kirby's Wonderful and Scientific Museum*

It was also rumoured that Graham was now considering moving house, either due to the hostile reaction of the community or his own embarrassment.[33]

Trial and Punishment

The public gallery of London's Old Bailey was packed early on 13 January 1804 when Francis Smith stood trial for the murder of Thomas Millwood. Smith looked dejected throughout the trial, appearing genteel and dressed in black. His face was pale and he at times found it hard to support himself. He was on trial for his life. If found guilty, he would be sentenced to death. And given that he'd already confessed to shooting Millwood, he was indeed guilty. Evidence was given by William Girdler, the watchman who had nearly arrested the ghost on 29 December and who had planned with Smith to catch the phantom. Millwood's sister, Anne, also told her story. When Francis Smith finally spoke in his defence, he was tongue-tied and his voice faltered. He addressed the jury:

> When the man came up whom I took for the ghost, and made no answer after I had called twice, but still advanced, I was so much alarmed that I did not know what to do. I drew the trigger inadvertently, without being sensible of what I was doing.[34]

A large number of character witnesses spoke on behalf of Smith, attesting to his honesty and humaneness. The spectators in the Old Bailey were sympathetic to the young defendant, as it seems were the jury. However, the Judge Lord Chief Baron MacDonald in summing up noted that even if Smith had been flustered when he fired his gun, he had still deliberately gone out with a deadly weapon ready to kill, something he had no right to do – even if he had shot the person who was pretending to be a ghost. The jury retired to deliberate Smith's fate. Smith himself became faint and was escorted outside for fresh air.

When Smith came back to the courtroom, he was 'perfectly benumbed and totally deprived of his senses.' After being out for over an hour, the jury returned to deliver their verdict – manslaughter. However, the judge rejected this verdict. Smith was on trial for murder, so only a verdict of guilty or not guilty of that crime could be returned. The jury retired for a few more minutes of deliberation. When they returned a second time, Smith struggled to his feet to hear their verdict: guilty of murder. Smith collapsed in stupefied despair and the Judge sentenced him to be executed the following Monday and his body to be given over to dissection.[35]

Smith was taken to Newgate prison to await his punishment. However, the same evening mercy was shown and Smith's sentence was eventually commuted to one year in prison.[36] He received a pardon from the king and was released the following July, having served seven months.[37]

Epilogue

At the end of January, there was another twist in the story. Another real Hammersmith Ghost had been found, according to the *Oracle and Daily Advertiser*. It was reported that three young men were walking home after a convivial evening when they caught someone playing at being a ghost. We are not told who the guilty party was, though it is hinted that he was an important and respected person. The 'gravity of his manners' meant that he had been beyond suspicion of playing such a prank, and the press referred to the culprit as a 'large grey jackass'. The word 'grey' seems to be a hint as to the posh ghost's identity, and would perhaps have been obvious to contemporary readers, but it leaves us with something of a mystery.[38]

This alleged 'real' Hammersmith Ghost could be just rumour or gossip repeated uncritically by the press. In fact, according to the investigations of R.S. Kirby in his 1804 book *Kirby's Wonderful and Scientific Museum Volume 2*, several elements of the Hammersmith Ghost story were unfounded. The sightings in which the ghost had horns, glowing eyes or could breathe fire were, he asserted, made up by the press, as was the tale of the Ghost scaring a coach driver and unharnessing his horses. The tragic story of the pregnant lady who had taken to her bed and died after being scared by the Ghost was also untrue. A pregnant woman had been scared, but by a drunk not a ghost, and she had not died.[39]

The press had certainly uncritically reported gossip and rumour in the case of the Hammersmith Ghost (nothing new there), and they certainly embellished and invented stories of their own. But, also, there really *was* a person – or perhaps more likely there were several individuals – impersonating a ghost to prank their neighbours and friends. This activity of 'playing the ghost' was endemic in Britain throughout the nineteenth and early twentieth centuries, and newspapers tended to view these episodes with aloof disdain that in those enlightened times, people were still so superstitious as to be scared by a prankster in a bed sheet. At the same time, though, the press couldn't resist sensationalist headlines about ghosts wandering the churchyards and lanes, and tone would veer from sanctimonious to jocular. Within days of the fatal shooting of Thomas Millwood, the press were back to making jokes. One anonymous columnist in the *Oracle and Daily Advertiser* quipped, 'The Hammersmith Ghost has produced one good effect, by rendering the labourers in the vicinity decidedly averse to spirits!' John Graham, the columnist continued, was so frightened at being caught that he has 'given up the Ghost!'[40]

As for John Graham, it seems he struggled to shake off his reputation as the 'Ghost'. When he was arrested for being drunk and disorderly more than thirty years later, the newspapers still referred to him as the Hammersmith Ghost. Graham and a friend had been walking home from the pub late one January night in 1837 when they saw two policemen escorting a prostitute they had arrested back to the station and with drunken gallantry decided to intervene, getting themselves both arrested in the process. At the trial, Graham was described as a 'bald-pated, grey-headed, old man' with a whining voice who tried to convince the judge that he was both pious and abstemious in the extreme. One newspaper referred to him as the 'Hammersmith Ghost – a spiritual drunkard'.[41] Three decades after the Hammersmith Ghost panic, the press still referred to John Graham sarcastically as 'his ghostship', demonstrating the enduring impact the events of winter 1803 and 1804 had on the populace.

Chapter Two

The Hammersmith Monster

> **'She was no little affrighted to behold in the doorway a strangely and "ghostly" dressed figure with a large ugly mask and glaring eye-balls. Some flame was then emitted, after which the Ghost exclaimed "Goodnight, farewell" and decamped with supernatural rapidity...'**
>
> **(*Morning Herald, 30 December 1824*)**

Twenty years after the Hammersmith Ghost came the Hammersmith Monster. Every time he struck, he seemed to get bolder. Not content with just scaring people, he disfigured them with metallic hooks or claws attached to his hands, vomited fire, and could change the colour of his costume as if by magic. The good people of Hammersmith were not even safe in their own homes...

There's a Monster Coming...

In November 1824, the lanes of Hammersmith were again haunted by a strange presence. A white figure of 'theatrically appalling stature' was reported to loom out of the darkness of the country lanes, terrifying all who encountered it. In particular, lone women were most likely to come face to face with what the newspapers were calling the new Hammersmith Ghost, in reference to the tragic events of 1804. Unfortunately, most of the early encounters with this new ghost are lacking in detail. On Friday16 November an unnamed servant girl from the Angel pub on Angel Lane Hammersmith was so frightened by her encounter with the figure that her life was despaired of, and she was left suffering fits for some weeks after. Soon after, a 'hardworking man' was walking near Hammersmith water works when a figure in white leapt on his back and threw him to the ground before vanishing, leaving his victim with a broken arm. The neighbourhood was 'seriously alarmed', and several young men lay in wait to catch the miscreant in action. The sufferings of the servant girl from the Angel especially attracted a great deal of sympathy from the locals.[1]

All went quiet for a number of nights. However, in early December the apparition was seen again in the lanes connecting Hammersmith and Chiswick and then again in Angel Lane. The unfortunate servant girl was once again confronted by a mysterious apparition. The girl and a 'hardworking' woman named Chambers had walked up the lane from the pub on the evening of 3 December, and the girl was left alone for a few minutes. The towering figure in white appeared before her and crossed her path several times, and then the white costume it wore suddenly turned to black and the apparition vanished into the night. It was later speculated that some prankster had created a ghost costume that could be easily flipped between the white 'ghost' side and a black side to make it easier to escape. The terrified girl was taken home and suffered constant fits for four hours. It was assumed that the ghost was targeting the poor girl for some unknown reason, and there was a great deal of support for her, especially as, we are told, she had nearly been run over by a wagon a few weeks ago.[2]

However, as Christmas approached, events would turn more sinister and the Hammersmith Ghost would become the Hammersmith Monster.

The Ghost Becomes a Monster

The first two weeks of December were quiet, but late on Saturday 18 December, the ghost returned with a vengeance. The first encounter involved Mr Cooke, the son of a respectable coal merchant, who was on horseback near Beaver Lane in Hammersmith, not far from where a man had had his arm broken when the mysterious white figure had leapt onto his back a few weeks previously. In his 'disordered' account, Crooke said the ghost was more than human height and seemed to rise out of the ground with its arms 'enormously expanded'. Later the same evening a woman was found in a state of hysterics in the same area and had to be escorted to a nearby gentleman's house. She had encountered the Hammersmith Ghost, though no further details are given in press reports except that it was some time before the lady was able to go home.

However, it was the attack that occurred on Monday 20 December that led to the ghost being renamed 'Monster'. The assault was on an unnamed young woman at Turnham Green. The sinister figure appeared to have little hooks or metallic claws attached to his fingers, and with these, he tore at the woman's clothes, and then at her face. The woman was said to be 'sadly disfigured'.[3] Wearing a white sheet and scaring people was bad enough, but the sadistic assault with hooked fingers on a defenceless woman was something far worse. It was monstrous.

The word 'monster' would have a very peculiar resonance for the people of London, and this was why the press chose this appellation. It was in reference to the London Monster panic of 1788–1790. The London Monster was said to attack beautiful women with metallic claws, sharp knives attached to his knees, or other implements with which he would stab their thighs or buttocks. Sometimes he would ask a young woman to smell a nosegay he was carrying, and then jab her in the face with a blade hidden among the flowers. A hysterical monster mania swept through the capital with women scared to go out, and any man might find himself under suspicion of being the Monster. There were eruptions of lynch mob violence as vigilante groups patrolled the night streets hoping to win the substantial reward on offer for the Monster's capture. The attacks continued to escalate through 1790, though they stopped after the arrest of an artificial flower maker called Rhynwick Williams, who had been identified by one of his victims.

Although Rhynwick Williams went down in history as the London Monster, he was certainly not responsible for all of the Monster attacks and had several witnesses who testified that he was working with them during some of the key attacks. Furthermore, some of the attacks turned out to be hoaxes, and there was the possibility that clumsy thieves attempting to cut purses out of pockets may have been responsible for some of the cuts the victims received.[4] Nevertheless, the community needed a scapegoat, and that scapegoat was Rhynwick Williams.

Despite the nighttime vigils of stout youths hoping to win a reward of five guineas each, no similar scapegoat for the Hammersmith Monster scare could be found.[5]

Not yet.

Bawdy satirical print of the London Monster (Isaak Cruikshank, 1790)

Mrs White's Tale

The whole of Hammersmith was in alarm with women afraid to go out at night. The press claimed several women who had encountered the Monster had fallen into fits while others had been scratched or torn in the face. Furthermore, the dark lanes, lonely paths, and open fields of early nineteenth century Hammersmith meant it was easy for the Monster to evade capture. The Monster had grown bolder, progressing from scaring his victims to scratching them with hooks or claws. But it seems the people of Hammersmith were not even safe in their own homes for his sensational next appearance was his most audacious yet.

Mrs White was married to a gardener and lived in a cottage in Bradmore, Hammersmith. Just after Christmas Day, she came face to face with the Monster in her own house. It was reported in the *Morning Herald*:

> She was no little affrighted to behold in the doorway a strangely and "ghostly" dressed figure with a large ugly mask and glaring eye-balls. Some flame was then emitted, after which the Ghost exclaimed "Goodnight, farewell" and decamped with supernatural rapidity…[6]

This is the most detailed description of the Monster so far, and fire-breathing is a new addition to his repertoire. Fortunately for Mrs White, for some reason the Monster kept his hooks to himself and opted instead to politely wish her a good night.

But as the Monster's fame grew, a few brave souls stood up against him.

The Old Woman with the Lantern

One night early in the New Year, an old woman was walking on Angel Lane, where the servant girl had seen the ghost a few weeks earlier.

The streets being dark and lonely, the unnamed woman carried a lantern with her, though the quiet lanes would be shadowy and eerie, nonetheless. As she walked, she became aware of a ghostly moaning sound from behind her, followed by a mysterious figure ominously tapping her lantern. The woman, though, held her nerve and without looking to the right or the left, she kept on walking trying not to express any fear. 'You would not be base enough to hurt an old woman, would you?' she asked the figure. The Monster did not respond but continued to follow her, mincing, and prancing around in theatrical ghost-like fashion. When she approached some houses, the figure left her.[7]

Whoever the old woman with the lamp was, she had refused to be intimidated by the Monster.

The Apprentice's Tale

Another person to stand up to this mysterious phantom was the young apprentice of Mr Hammond Smith and Co. As with so many of the reports of the Hammersmith Monster, we are left without a name for the brave apprentice. Not long after the old woman's encounter, the apprentice was walking near Hammersmith waterworks along a lane next to some newly built houses. This is the border between rural Hammersmith, and the ever-expanding urban monster that was London, coming to devour it. It was also the site of a previous Monster attack that left a man with a broken arm. According to this unnamed apprentice, the ghostly figure seemed to rise up from the ground in front of him. He was a spirited lad, so he hurled the basket of tinned goods he was carrying at the Monster before grabbing its silky costume and attempting to pull it off. There was an intense tug-o-war between the two until the Monster dealt the apprentice a violent blow on the back of his head that sent him sprawling in the mud. The Monster made his escape and the apprentice was helped home by some residents who came to his aid.

Angry mob chase a 'ghost' in Devon

(*Illustrated Police News*, 29 September 1894)

The apprentice was reported to be reluctant to go out after dark for fear of feeling the 'heavy arm' of the Monster again. There was a further anonymous report of a man grabbing and grappling with 'ghosty' (as the press sometimes referred to the miscreant, always in ironic italics), and in this case the man was also knocked flat by the Monster's heavy arm.[8]

However, these incidents demonstrate that Ghost, Monster or ghosty – whoever he was, the people of Hammersmith were out to get him.

Monster Hunters in Drag

In a letter to a London newspaper, Mr W. Brown described how he had caught a 'ghost' in Poplar, East London and offered some advice to the Monster Hunters of Hammersmith. Brown wrote that a man dressed in a white sheet had been roaming Poplar at night and throwing stones at windows. One can imagine how spooky – not to say annoying – it would be to be awoken with the sound of a stone rattling against one's window, and then to look outside and see a ghostly figure staring back. Mr Brown and his friends stationed themselves around the ghost's haunts, and when he appeared they jumped on him:

> We immediately rushed upon him, and gave him such a whacking as ever he had in his life, and fortunately, the common sewer being near, we gave him a good ducking, and lodged him safe in the watch-house.[9]

When ghost hoaxers were caught red-handed in the nineteenth and early twentieth century, they would often face a sound thumping along with a dunking in any nearby river, canal – or sewer. Playing the ghost was risky business.

In his letter, Mr Brown advised the young men of Hammersmith to station themselves to watch for the Monster in his various haunts. However, the lads of Hammersmith went one step further. They dressed as women, hoping to lure the Monster into attacking them. This monster hunt in drag would surely have been seen as something of a boozy festive lark by the young bucks, and added to the sense of the carnivalesque that often accompanied these ghost panics. In any case, the Monster managed to resist the charms of the pantomime dame vigilantes and he remained at large. But not for long.

The Ghost Rider's Tale

On the evening of 15 February 1825, patrolman Mr N. Worsley was returning to Fulham from Kensington when he encountered a man draped in a white sheet on horseback. The 'ghost' had a hairy cap tied under his chin and, with arms outstretched, was uttering unearthly noises. Worsley sprang at the apparition and yanked off the white sheet, throwing it into a nearby garden. Worsley then pulled the man from his horse and a 'severe scuffle' ensued in which the 'ghost' thumped the patrolman in the face with the butt of his whip. At this point another man named Joseph Salter came out of a nearby house and told Worsley not to interfere as it was only a bit of a 'lark'. However, Worsley was determined to secure the man who had been haunting Hammersmith over the winter months, and luckily Isaac Hawkins, another nightwatchman, turned up at that moment. The 'ghost', whose name was John Benjamin, a local farmer and hay salesman, then accused Worsley of having stolen his sheet further saying that he would prosecute the watchmen for stealing two sovereigns from him in the struggle.[10] Benjamin, who was furious at his capture, and Salter were sent home with Benjamin being ordered to appear at the county magistrate's house the following day.

News of the capture of the supposed ghost spread fast. When John Benjamin appeared at magistrate Mr Hanson's house in Hammersmith the next day, all the surrounding roads and lanes were thronged with people hoping to catch a glimpse of the 'ghost' that had been haunting them for the past months. The crowds were such that the roads became impassible.[11]

John Benjamin was said to be a respectable farmer and pork butcher. He told Mr Hanson that on the night he had been caught he had taken some pig carcases to market wrapped in large white sheets. Having received payment for these, and spending some of the money in the pub, he was rather drunk, though still stopped to distribute some of the sheets to a mission for fallen women on his way back. It was then that he had the drunken idea to 'play the ghost' and wrap one of the sheets around himself.

However, a night patrolman named James Silverthorne happened to be on duty walking past the White Hart pub shortly before Benjamin was caught. He heard loud laughter coming from inside the pub doorway, so Silverthorne and his partner decided to investigate. Silverthorne's partner went in and bought a beer and while supping it he saw Benjamin and Slater at the bar. The watchmen saw Benjamin take a large white cloth from a draw behind the bar, though the landlady begged him not to. Benjamin said it would cover his horse's rump, and then wrapped it around his shoulders. Silverthorne said to Benjamin that if he went out with the sheet over him, it could lead to him 'having his brains beat out', though Benjamin took no notice and rode into the night with the sheet wrapped around him. He was discovered by Worsley soon after moaning and cavorting as a ghost. It didn't look good for Benjamin, and he faced a misdemeanour charge for 'disguising himself so as to alarm his Majesty's subjects.'[12]

'Pork butcher could not save his bacon', one newspaper could not resist quipping.[13]

Epilogue

It's not clear what happened to John Benjamin, though it appears he received some kind of custodial sentence. As one newspaper put it, 'he was sent by the Magistrates to the House of Correction to undergo a little wholesome discipline for his pranks.'[14] However, it's very likely that Benjamin wasn't the Ghost/Monster that had been stalking the lanes of Hammersmith, and may only have donned his ghostly disguise the once while he was in his cups. Although the press assumed that Benjamin was responsible for all the attacks, this is implausible. There are several obvious differences between Benjamin's prank and the various reported encounters with the Hammersmith Monster. Benjamin didn't physically attack anyone (except for the watchman who had accosted him). Furthermore, he didn't breathe fire, have metallic hooks on his hands or a magic colour changing cloak. Finally, unlike in all the other reported encounters, he was on a horse. As was the case with the London Monster panic of 1790, it sometimes takes a scapegoat to burst the bubble of a ghost panic.

We should entertain the possibility that some escapades with the Ghost/Monster were hoaxes carried out by the supposed victims. Some of the purported attacks are reminiscent of the Halifax Slasher scare that occurred in November 1938, where residents of the West Yorkshire town were terrorised by a razor blade wielding maniac. It later transpired that the many victims had inflicted the injuries on themselves – to get attention or sympathy, to get revenge on boyfriends or due to their 'nerves' – and invented stories of a mad assailant.[15] These episodes where an anxious community is terrorised by an imaginary attacker are rather common and are sometimes known as Phantom Attacker panics. Perhaps this is what happened in Hammersmith. The accounts of the servant girl from the Angel pub who was attacked twice might be viewed with some scepticism – there were no previous reports of the ghost having metal claws – and the fact that she claimed to have been attacked twice raises some doubts in my mind. Similarly, the appearance of the fire-breathing apparition in Mrs White's house seems somewhat suspicious. In fact, many of the reports may have been invented by the victims as rumours of the Hammersmith Ghost/Monster spread. It's also noteworthy that the vast majority of reports lack details such as the name of the victim, and so the press may have exaggerated, conflated and even invented some of the episodes.

This doesn't discount the strong possibility that there were one or more ghost hoaxers at play; there clearly were, with John Benjamin being one of them. Suspicion also fell on an unnamed gentleman who had gone around Hammersmith chalking dire warnings on people's gates and doors. The messages included 'Prepare to die!', 'Your end is near!' and 'Ye are all lost sinners.' However, this gentleman was really too old to be a fake ghost. To successfully scare people and then disappear requires some agility on the ghost's part.[16]

Another rumour that did the rounds was that the Ghost/ Monster was actually a nobleman's son who had wagered that he could 'walk as a ghost' around the streets of Hammersmith for a number of nights without being caught. However, it was believed that he had been captured in Kensington in late January, though his being of noble kin meant the story was hushed up. This is little more than a rumour, though it was indeed a common trope at the time that the sons of aristocrats were amusing themselves in this manner at the expense of the common people, and possibly there was some truth in the claim that young bloods might get up to such mischief. This was again rumoured when the Hammersmith Ghost reappeared briefly over the winter of 1833, this time wearing a large white dress and sporting long nails or claws supposedly to allow him to effect his quick escape by climbing over walls and hedges. The culprit was said to be a 'captain of sporting notoriety' who had taken on a wager that he could strip a certain number of women of their clothes.[17]

In 1838, a highly fictionalised version of the Hammersmith Ghost story appeared in *Fraser's Magazine for Town and Country*.[18] It tells the story of Julian, a boy so attractive that he was stolen by gypsies and then sold to a duchess as a toy boy. However, he's so handsome that ladies everywhere just can't help throwing themselves at him and, after killing a man in a duel, he flees to Italy. There, his good looks continue to cause trouble as a lady poisons herself after being refused by him and he is sent to prison as an accomplice in her suicide. After forty years in prison, he escapes by seducing the warden's daughter and returns to Hammersmith. His beauty, though, is undiminished by age, and London women continue to throw themselves into his arms to such a degree that he takes to wandering the lanes of Hammersmith at night dressed in a white and black costume, giving rise to the ghostly rumours that spread through the district. The story makes several references to the events of 1803 and 1804, though in this retelling, the 'ghost' is simply trying to avoid female attention rather than to scare innocent people. The story ends farcically when Julian dresses as a knight in armour for no apparent reason and on one of his nocturnal walks rescues what he thinks is a beautiful heiress imprisoned in a tower and is chased by her guardian and the police. When the heiress turns out to be a maid called Sally, he dumps her with the police and makes his escape.

As we have seen, Hammersmith appears to have been particularly bothered with ghost hoaxing in the early nineteenth century. Perhaps it's because at the time it was a place where London urbanisation was encroaching on rural areas. As Jacob Middleton notes, anyone pretending to be a ghost in an urban area was more likely to be caught due to a larger population to give chase and better lighting. However, ghost hoaxing in rural areas offers easy means of escape into fields or woods, but it's harder to find anyone to scare. Hammersmith in the early nineteenth century was the perfect environment for a ghost hoax. There were urban areas where it would be possible for ghosts to find an 'audience', and there were dark, narrow lanes to disappear into.[19] Hammersmith was a place between two worlds – the rural and the urban – and in folklore borders between worlds are seen as strange and magical places, and weird things happen there.

Spring-Heeled Jack from an English penny dreadful (c.1860)

Chapter Three

The Peterborough Poltergeist

'... it went on nightly for nearly a week, the lumberings up and down our bedroom passage were dreadful, and the bedroom doors open and shut violently. It was frightful...'

(Mrs Rimes, 1892)

In the Christmas and New Year period of 1892, a railway worker's family and their neighbours in Peterborough were haunted by strange, unearthly sounds. Invisible hands would pull off bedclothes and doors would bang and rattle. However, it was the terrifying noise that came from the passage outside their bedrooms that scared the family the most. Sceptical investigators who stayed overnight in the house soon regretted it, and rumours spread about mysterious lights, spirit messages, witchcraft, and a blazing red and black hell-hound. There is, though, more than one twist in the true tale of the Peterborough Poltergeist...

The Peterborough Ghost

When the Rimes family took on the lease of 22 Mayor's Walk, Peterborough in 1891, it became a rather crowded household. There was Mr Rimes, a railway worker who was often away from home for nights at a time, and his wife Mrs Rimes, described as a strong and cheerful woman in her mid-forties. As well as their three children, there were also Mrs Rime's brother Mr Want and her brother-in-law Mr Easy who lodged with them. Want and Easy were also railway workers like Mr Rimes. Mayor's Walk was one of several cottages occupied by railwaymen and their families on the west side of Peterborough adjacent to the Midland Railway. Number 22 had three bedrooms, meaning the Rimes' three young boys shared a room with either Want or Easy or their parents.[1] By Christmas 1891, the house would be the focus of intense speculation by the local population. By the New Year, it gained national notoriety as the home of the Peterborough Ghost.

The first strange occurrence in the Rimes' residence was around Halloween, 1891. Mrs Rimes had gone to bed at around 11pm when she heard Arthur, her middle son, shout 'Did you come into my room just now, mother?' She replied that she hadn't, though at breakfast the following morning Arthur asked his mother if she was sure she hadn't entered his room during the night. When she assured him that she hadn't, Arthur replied, 'Mother, I am sure someone did.' At this point, Mrs Rimes thought he was talking nonsense, but Arthur was adamant that someone had entered his room. One night later Mrs Rimes was woken by the terror-stricken shrieks of two of her children who had been sleeping next to her. They said that something – an invisible hand – had pulled the bedclothes off them. Mrs Rimes tried to convince the children this was impossible, but her own confidence that the children had imagined the episode must have been shaken by what her brother had previously told her. Furthermore, Mr Want also said he had felt someone or something pull the bedclothes from the bed.[2]

As Christmas approached other odd things disturbed the household. Doors would knock and rattle, sometimes violently, as though someone were outside shaking the handle and attempting to get in. Whenever Mrs Rimes opened the door, nobody was to be seen. Sometimes when Mr Want (Mrs Rimes's brother) heard the door banging at night, he would cry out 'Halloa! Come inside and let's see what you are.' The knocking would cease as abruptly as it started.[3] On one occasion the shaking of the door handle was enough to break the door.[4] Mysterious coloured lights would dance around the living room in the hours of darkness.[5] Rumours spread through the town that one night Mrs Rimes had seen a flaming red and black demonic hound come down the chimney.[6]

However, the Friday before Christmas 1891 was the most frightening so far. Shortly before two in the morning, a weird humming noise began. This was followed by loud knockings in the corridor that connected the three upstairs bedrooms, as if someone were stamping along the passage with an unearthly tread, louder than could be produced by any normal means. Everyone jumped out of bed and ran to investigate but the noise stopped and nothing was to be seen in the passage. As soon as they returned to bed the horrendous noises began again. The nerves of Mrs Rimes, her children and the two lodgers were so frazzled by what they heard that they gave up on sleep and went and sat downstairs desperate for daylight to come.[7]

The noises in the corridor were so loud that neighbours on both sides of 22 Mayor's Walk were able to hear it. Mr Butler at number 21 described the noise as like 'a giant tearing up a kitchen table and hurling the pieces down the stairs, or like the clattering of slates.' Meanwhile, on the other side, Mrs Goode at number 23 was sewing a button onto some clothing in the early hours when she heard the noise, which she described as being like a cannon that was so violently loud that it shook the whole house. She ran and hid under the covers of her bed.[8]

These noises continued night after night. Mrs Rimes told the press:

> Well, it went on nightly for nearly a week, the lumberings up and down our bedroom passage were dreadful, and the bedroom doors open and shut violently. It was frightful; none of us slept.[9]

The corridor from where the noises seemed to originate was termed the 'Ghost Walk' by the terrified family. They would sleep with the doors open, and move their beds into position such that they could see anyone who entered the passage, but whenever the heavy footsteps, knocking or crashing occurred, there was no one there. The family were sure that none of them was playing a prank on the others as the noises often occurred when they were all together in one room, too scared to sleep. Mr Easy, Mrs Rimes's brother-in-law, thought the noises were somehow meant for him. His wife had died a year ago, and he wondered if she was trying to contact him from beyond the grave.[10]

In any case, the residents of 22 Mayor's Walk were distressed, baffled and sleep-deprived. It was time to call in someone who knew about these things – a Ghost Detective.

The Ghost Detective's Tale

The investigator was Mr Arthur Wright and, although the press reports referred to him as a private detective, he was actually employed at a local railway goods shed.[11] It seems that Mr Wright was something of a sceptic regarding ghostly matters, having exposed several imposters playing at being ghosts.[12] He knew Mr Want and Mr Easy and told them he didn't believe in their ghost. Nevertheless, he agreed to stay the night and witness the noises for himself.

Plan of 22 Mayor's Walk (*Buckinghamshire Advertiser*, 16 January 1892)

Accordingly, on the night before New Year's Eve, the intrepid ghostbuster arrived at 22 Mayor's Walk. He checked that all the doors and windows were locked to ensure nobody could enter or leave the house without him knowing about it, then settled down and waited...[13]

A few minutes after midnight, he heard a peculiar humming sound. This was followed by a tapping coming from the passage, causing Mr Wright to shout 'Hallo! Your [sic] here again are you', before dashing into the corridor known as the Ghost Walk. All was quiet and everyone was in bed. Just as he settled down again, Wright heard an unearthly noise that he described as like a sack of coals being thrown down the stairs. 'The noise was awful' he told the press. 'I can't explain it, I don't care to think of it.' He rushed to the staircase to investigate, but nothing unusual was to be seen. He checked the bedrooms and saw the children were still in their beds. However, the noise had now woken the whole household, and they were as terrified as Mr Wright. As they all stood together in the same room, more knocks and thumps could be heard. The neighbours also lost sleep. Mr Butler at number 21 described the noise as being akin to 'the fall of a house into the passage.' Mrs Goode at number 23 said it was 'like the explosion of a great gun which shook the house and all in it. The noise before it was like that when a boy rubs the string of his toy telephone.'

There would be no more sleep that night for any of the residents of the Rimes household. They sat downstairs around the kitchen fire until first light, and then Mr Wright left at the earliest opportunity, his scepticism severely shaken.[14]

It was also the last straw for the Rimes family. They moved out early in the New Year and number 22 Mayor's Walk stood empty.

But not for long...

We Are Going to Peterborough to Find the Ghost

Shortly after the house became vacant on 15 January 1892, the Chief Constable of Peterborough received a telegram signed by one Scrimshaw of 5 Babbington Street, Nottingham. It read 'Will you allow three experts to stay in the supposed haunted house next Monday?' The Chief assumed that the 'experts' were scientific gentlemen from the Society for Psychical Research, so he agreed.[15] Scrimshaw telegrammed again, saying, 'Please say if the mystery is fathomed. If so, no use our coming.' The Chief informed them that the ghost appeared to have left when the Rimes moved out. Undeterred, Scrimshaw replied saying 'We shall arrive at 15:15, Monday.' The telegram was signed 'Ghost'. Scrimshaw later sent a letter to the Chief Constable explaining that he and his team of experts were investigating because of the great deal of public interest in the case, though he warned the policeman not to let the public know they were coming.[16]

The Chief Constable assumed that these scientific gentlemen would call at the police station before commencing their investigation, but when they didn't show up he became suspicious. He went to 22 Mayor's Walk and was surprised to see a boy enter the house carrying a jug of beer. He followed the boy inside to find three men in blue coats, uniforms that suggested they were butchers. They were sitting in front of a roaring fire and had clearly been 'enjoying their pipe and glass' as they had attempted to transform themselves into turbaned mystics by swaddling their heads and necks in towels. The Chief asked the three rather drunk men how they had got into the house, and they told him they'd borrowed the key from the neighbour.

At this point, the new tenant showed up and he was not at all happy to find a party of drunk turbaned butchers in his house. He told them to 'clear out', though they asked to stay until Scrimshaw's 'agent' Mr Barr arrived. Barr soon arrived, and just as the group were being turned out, the enigmatic

Mr Scrimshaw appeared having been into town to arrange for some supper for the 'investigators'. It seems the party had made a bet or a dare that they could stay overnight in the haunted house in Peterborough. They had even decorated the train carriage they travelled down from Nottingham in with a sign saying 'We are going to Peterborough to find the Ghost.' We don't know how much they had staked on their bet, but they lost.[17]

The Stranger's Tale

In early January a journalist from the *Peterborough Express* went to interview the Rimes's neighbours and other locals about the ghostly occurrences. They all ridiculed the story, and said it was just playful banter, though a few individuals who were of a somewhat nervous disposition had been alarmed. As the journalist was asking people about the ghost, he was approached by a stranger who was identified only as 'a Great Northern Railway Employee', who asked of the reporter, 'Talking about the ghost, are you? Why, it's gone, and I saw it go on New Year's Eve.'

The stranger said that he had been walking home on New Year's Eve shortly before midnight, and as he passed Mayor's Walk, a man jumped out on him before dashing off into the surrounding fields. Because the man did not say goodnight, and behaved so suspiciously, the railway employee concluded that this man was the prankster responsible for the ghostly noises. Furthermore, he knew who he was, though didn't reveal this to the journalist.

The railway employee further explained that the prankster had created the 'ghost' by rattling doors and throwing large rocks onto the roof of the house. The rocks rolled and bounced down the roof before crashing into the ground, giving the impression of footsteps thudding along the passage and other unearthly noises. Other strange sounds, the stranger believed, were caused by the Rimes's family pets – a dog and a cat. The animals were not put out at night, and it's certainly conceivable that a cat tearing around the house in the early hours as they are wont to do might have contributed to the strange noises. The pets may also have been responsible for pulling the bedclothes off the sleeping family. The mysterious coloured lights seen in the house were caused, the stranger believed, by red and green railway signals shining far up the line directly into 22 Mayor's Walk. The stranger said he was certainly not scared of anything in the house and would happily spend the night there – if he was paid.[18]

As for the demonic black and red flaming hound that had supposedly come down the chimney, Mrs Rimes herself dismissed that as a baseless rumour. It had come about when the son-in-law of her neighbours the Goodes had knocked on their back door and saw through the window a black dog jump up in the air and then not show itself again. As this story was retold among neighbours and locals, the episode gained dramatic extra colour until a fire breathing red and black hell hound burst from the chimney.[19]

W.T. Stead's Tale

In February 1892, the *Peterborough Standard* wrote, 'and now the bogey has served its little newspaper-selling purpose it is probable that it will be relegated to the limbo of forgetfulness.'[20] However, it was at this juncture that one of Britain's most infamous newspaper editors and Spiritualist W.T. Stead became involved. Stead was a pioneer of tabloid style journalism, even having spent time in prison for purchasing a child in order to demonstrate that this practice was common in London in his famous 'Maiden Tribute of Modern Babylon' campaign against child prostitution.[21] His sensational articles resulted in the age of consent for girls being raised from 13 to 16, the law coming to be known as the Stead Act. In the 1880s, along with many scientists and intellectuals of the time, he became fascinated by Spiritualism and mediums, and this interest led to him writing to the *Peterborough Express* about the supposed ghost at 22 Mayor's Walk.

Stead proposed that he form a team to investigate the house. His plan was to collaborate with George Edward Gourard, an American Civil War veteran and the man who introduced Edison's phonographic cylinder to England in 1888. It was hoped that they would be able to obtain a recording of the Peterborough Ghost. This would be a ghost hunt making use of the very latest in modern technology.

W.T. Stead (E.H. Mills, London)

Stead received a reply from the newspaper saying that the cottage was now being rented out at £12 per annum by the manager of the *Express*, but that investigators would be allowed access for the sum of £7 and 10 shillings per night. The reply also informed Stead that the phenomena only occurred when Mr Rimes was in the house, and that he too would require a fee. Stead abandoned his plan in despair, noting that the presence of a ghost served to raise the rent from £12 a year to over £7 a night.[22]

Epilogue

When the Rimes, their lodgers and their cat and dog left 22 Mayor's Walk in early January 1892, the strange noises ceased altogether and were not heard again. Whether there was anything more to the ghost than a prankster rattling the doors and chucking rocks at the roof, signal lights shining through the windows and the nocturnal activities of peripatetic pets is hard to say. The residents would certainly have had their nerves on edge and would have been in a state of hypervigilance such that any bump or creak might be attributed to the ghost. The *Peterborough Standard* suggests that its rival paper the *Peterborough Express* was financially involved in the case either to sell newspapers with its sensational story or having an interest in renting the cottage to intrepid investigators.[23]

At Christmas 1893, one year after his unsuccessful attempt to investigate the Peterborough Ghost, W.T. Stead published a story called 'From the Old World to the New' about a huge transatlantic liner called the Majestic. Stead gave the Majestic's skipper the name of a real captain – Edward Smith. In the story a psychic passenger tells Captain Smith to change his course because he had a vision of an iceberg and a sinking ship. The real-life Captain Edward Smith, of course, went on to become skipper of the ill-fated Titanic. In a strange example of life imitating art, W.T. Stead was one of the 1,500 or so souls who perished when the Titanic hit an iceberg and sank below the Atlantic in 1912. He was last seen heroically giving his lifebelt to another passenger.[24]

Stead supposedly wrote a book from beyond the grave called *The Blue Island: Experiences of a New Arrival Beyond the Veil,* in which he detailed his adventures in the afterlife to Spiritualist medium Woodman Pardoe, though that is another story.[25]

Chapter Four

The Christmas Churchyard Riot ~ The Islington Ghost

'On Christmas night, while passing the old parish church, I was startled by seeing a figure in white standing in front of me. I stopped, when it seemed to vanish towards the church...'
(James Chant, letter to *Islington Gazette, 1899*)

On Christmas Day 1899, a man claimed to have seen a ghost haunting the graveyard of Saint Mary's parish church, Islington. There soon followed a riotous ghost hunt among the tombs as thousands gathered in the hope of seeing the ghost, or at least to have disorderly larks in the graveyard. Police, however, suspected the whole episode was part of a cunning plot by devious criminals...

Mr Chant's Tale

On 3 January 1899, the *Islington Gazette* published a letter from a Mr James Chant of 223 Essex Road.[1] The letter claimed that on Christmas night Mr Chant was passing Saint Mary's parish church in Islington when he witnessed something strange:

> On Christmas night, while passing the old parish church, I was startled by seeing a figure in white standing in front of me. I stopped, when it seemed to vanish towards the church. It didn't go in a gliding way, as spooks generally do, but in a very clumsy manner. I made for him but he was too quick.

Later that evening Chant returned to the churchyard and met another man who said he had also seen the mysterious pale figure. At this moment, both men again saw the 'ghost' on the other side of the railings and gave chase, but failed to catch up with it.

In the letter, Chant went on to say that the ghost 'has often been seen there about eight of an evening' and that he suspected it was someone playing a Christmas joke, yet he found it hard to understand how the figure could escape so fast or where it disappeared to. Furthermore, Chant offered the following speculation:

> If this is an old resident of Islington coming back to this world again to pay a visit to his old friends, I shall be most happy to shake hands with him and drink his health, for I intend going up there to wait upon him and also my friend.

St Mary's Church Islington (G. Newcombe 1843)

The following day the *Islington Gazette* published a sceptical commentary on Chant's letter.[2] The unnamed author wrote that reports of churchyard ghosts are often invented by hoaxers hoping to create a sensation and draw a crowd. The article also asked why James Chant was in the vicinity of a churchyard on Christmas night, commenting that dyspepsia can cause the sufferer to see optical illusions. It was noted that Chant claimed that the ghost had been seen frequently, and yet there had been no gathering of crowds at the churchyard. As we see in the other stories in this book, rumours of ghosts frequently resulted in crowds of the curious gathering at the location of the supposed haunting – the ghost hunting flash mob. The *Gazette* argued that it was highly unusual for no mob to congregate around a wonder like a supposed ghost. As an example of public gullibility, the paper recalled that Irish playwright Joseph Brinsley Sheridan had caused huge crowds to gather around Northumberland House in the Strand when he declaimed in a loud voice that he had seen the stone lion that tops the building wag its tail.

In any case, Chant's letter was practically an invitation to a ghost hunt, and that is what ensued.

A Vulgar Riot

The *Islington Gazette* was completely wrong about crowds not gathering around the churchyard, at least when it came to the following evening. By midnight the crowd was five hundred strong, and, according to the press, was comprised mostly of 'roughs'. The shouts and catcalls from the 'disorderly mob' attracted passing pedestrians who also joined the crowds around the churchyard. The police were called and attempted to stop passers-by from joining the throng, but this only made things worse – if five hundred people have spontaneously assembled to see something and the police want to stop you from seeing it, then it must be something really worth seeing. As more and more gathered looking for the ghost, more police were sent to try to control what the newspapers called a 'vulgar riot'.

Many of the curious who went to try to see the ghost found they came back with their watch or purse missing. Several respectable people were 'molested in a disgraceful way' or 'hustled' and there were a few minor injuries.[3] Although we don't get many details about what happened in the newspapers, it's obvious that they thoroughly disapproved of the 'roughs' and their behaviour. Interestingly, the press reports frequently compared the Islington Ghost episode to similar events in London churchyards over the previous decades, and these accounts give us an idea of what these ghost hunts were like.

The Islington churchyard 'vulgar riot' was most often compared to the Hackney ghost scare of 1895 by the press, so we can look at this episode to get a picture of what happened in Islington. The churchyard of St John's, Hackney, had a ghost legend attached to it. At the back of the church was a gravestone with a sculpture or a carving of three boys playing cards on a table. The legend goes that this image refers to a true event. Three boys were playing cards for money and one was losing heavily. He said, 'May God strike me dead if I do not win this game.' After this blasphemous challenge, the boy stood up from the table and promptly dropped dead. It is the ghost of this boy that was said to wander Hackney's churchyard.[4]

In late August 1895 rumours spread in Hackney that a white figure had been seen flitting between the graves in the churchyard, and crowds of ghost hunters began to gather in the evenings of the next few days. Sometimes the crowd numbered several thousand often carrying lanterns, candles and sticks and stones, climbing over the railings and trampling on the graves. Jokers kept shouting 'There it goes!' instigating wild goose chases among the tombstones accompanied by horseplay and japes as well as scuffles, assaults, and the picking of pockets. People hid behind gravestones making hideous or otherworldly noises, and at times the effect was heightened dramatically by the lightning of a summer storm illuminating the gloom of the graveyard. The noise was so great that choir practice inside the church had to be abandoned. The police tried to move the crowds on, but to farcical effect. The churchyard had several entrances and every time the ghost hunters were ushered or manhandled out of one by the police, they just returned through another gate.[5]

The press claimed that the riotous ghost hunts in Hackney all started with a joke that was misunderstood by a journalist. An unnamed woman had complained to a reporter about not being able to sleep because of the heat. She told the journalist – as a joke – that she had looked out of her window and seen a white figure flitting between the trees of Hackney churchyard. The implication was that it was so hot that even the dead couldn't sleep. This joke taken literally led to reports of ghostly activity in the churchyard and the carnivalesque mob that descended soon after. Several newspapers suggested the woman had actually seen a lady dressed in light clothes being escorted home past the churchyard and mistaken this for a ghost.[6]

Hackney churchyard ghost hunt (*Illustrated Police News*, 31 August 1895)

Churchyard ghost hunts like that of Hackney in 1895 and Islington in 1899 happened quite frequently over the nineteenth century.[7] The one that happened in Islington would have been very similar to the Hackney affair. These ghost hunts were very different from the staid investigations of the psychic researchers or the whimsical Spiritualists. Many of the Islington ghost hunters will have prepared for the evening's hunt in the pub, and the shenanigans in the churchyard would resemble a boozy impromptu party with prank scares and people chasing each other around the gravestones. The press certainly viewed these high jinks with middle class disdain for the riotous fun of the masses. There was something transgressive and disrespectful of authority in these lairy ghost hunts, and it suggests that many saw ghost rumours not with the superstitious dread that the haughty press attributed to them, but more as an excuse for boozy larks in the dark.

Epilogue

There was speculation that the Islington ghost scare was deliberately fabricated to entice a large crowd of drunken revellers who would be easy prey for pickpockets in the dark of the graveyard. As the Islington scare began with a letter by James Chant, it wasn't long before reporters went in search of him. When a journalist from the *Islington Gazette*, which had published the letter about the Christmas ghost, called at 223 Essex Road the landlady informed him that nobody of the name James Chant resided there, although she had received a number of letters addressed to the elusive Mr Chant, as well as for a Mr Grisdale and a Mr Hanbury. All of these she returned to the post office. The landlady professed that she did not believe in ghosts and thought someone had been pranking her.

It seems implausible that the landlady herself would have been responsible for the hoax letter. If the landlady had wanted to play a joke, it's unlikely that she would have used a false name and yet still have given her real address. It's certainly plausible that an unscrupulous pickpocket came up with the cunning stratagem of sending a fake letter to the press using a random address with the deliberate intention of starting the ghost rumour in order to pick a few pockets as the crowds full of Christmas spirit hustled and jostled each other in the dark. The police certainly entertained the theory that sometimes criminal gangs did start these kinds of ghost panics to exploit the disorderly crowd and relieve them of their wallets and watches.[8] If this was the plan, the Christmas ghost of Islington graveyard certainly served its purpose.

Picture 10 St Mary's (John Salmon)

Chapter Five

Spring-Heeled Jack ~ The Lochee Ghost

'In front of her stood an awful vision dressed in white... His hat was ablaze with light, and, as the breeze blew the folds of his garments aside, it disclosed vestments of flaming red...'

(Dundee Evening Post, 22 December 1900)

Christmas 1900 saw a strange ghost haunting the streets of Lochee, Dundee. His bizarre white and red clothing and his distinctive hat that shone with an unearthly light caused panic among the inhabitants as more and more of them came face to face with this weird, menacing spectacle. However, it was not just the 'Ghost' that anxious residents had to be concerned about – it was also the disturbing effect that fear, suspicion and anxiety can have on a community in the grip of a ghost panic...

The Princesses' Tale

There is a darkly romantic prelude to the Lochee Ghost's exploits over the Christmas period of 1900. It begins not in Scotland but in India.

Fletcher Read was a high-ranking officer in the military service with the East India Company, and his position involved meeting with Indian dignitaries and their families. At one of these functions Fletcher became enamoured with Princess Kalee, a beautiful and free-spirited daughter of a prince. He asked the prince for permission to marry Kalee, but as she was his favourite daughter, the prince was reluctant to give his blessing, even though Kalee had also fallen in love with Fletcher. To persuade the prince to consent, Fletcher promised to take care of his daughter as if she were a child in a cradle.

The prince finally agreed to the wedding and threw in his daughter's weight in gold and diamonds as a wedding present. But first, Fletcher had to put his signature to the promise he had made to care for the Princess as if she were a child in a cradle. On the prince's insistence, Fletcher signed the promise with his own blood.

Fletcher and Kalee eventually moved to Scotland to live in Fletcher's mansion, the House of Logie near the town of Lochee, on the outskirts of Dundee. Although Kalee loved her husband and bore him two children, he soon tired of her company and eventually grew to despise her. Cruelly, the Laird banished his wife to a small house in a lonely hollow on his estate where she was confined to a dungeon. The house in which the unfortunate princess was imprisoned was said to be shaped somewhat like a cradle, therefore enabling the wicked Laird to claim that he had kept his promise to the prince to care for his daughter as if she were in a cradle.

Kalee died in her confinement, though some accounts say she was murdered by her husband. However, Fletcher did not know that Kalee had been in correspondence with a mysterious Indian gentleman who had been sent as a spy by her family to see that she was treated as befits a woman of her status. When it was made known that the princess had died, the mysterious Indian gentleman disappeared.

Sometime later, Fletcher received a letter from India. It said that the prince, his father-in-law, had passed away and that he was now entitled to a huge fortune. Fletcher journeyed to India and was met by members of Kalee's family with great pomp and circumstance, a welcome that no doubt flattered the Laird. However, Fletcher was surprised when he was taken deeper and deeper into the interior of the country. It was there in some remote spot that the royal family enacted its revenge on Fletcher by slowly torturing him to death.

Logie House (from *Lochee as it was and is* by Alexander Elliot, 1911)

There are several tangled versions of this legendary tale, and historically there are some issues with it. The main problem is that although Fletcher Read was indeed a real person, it seems he never went to India and died choking on his own vomit after a riotous night out in Scotland, rather than being slowly murdered in India.

Nevertheless, a ramshackle whitewashed ruin known as the 'Cradle of Logie' stood in a gloomy hollow surrounded by a cluster of looming pines near the road to Lochee. Children would be too scared to walk past the ruins as it was said that ghost of the tragic Indian princess haunted the environs. She was called 'the Dark Lady of Logie'.[1]

By the middle of the nineteenth century, Lochee was a bustling weaving town that had in a short time seen its population quadruple as Irish immigrants escaping the devastating potato famine came seeking work. The town gained the nickname of 'Little Tipperary' and by 1859 had been officially incorporated into the expanding city of Dundee.[2]

'Little Tipperary', Lochee, Dundee

And this brings us to Christmas 1900, and the story of Spring Heeled Jock – the Lochee Ghost.

The Lochee Ghost

On a December evening a young unnamed factory worker from Lochee went to visit her sister. When she was returning home and passing by the gloomy scene that legend said was where Fletcher Read had cruelly treated his Indian princess bride, the young woman's thoughts would likely have turned to that melancholy story and the rumours of Kalee's restless spirit. But as she looked over the hollow where the Cradle of Logie had stood, she saw a strange, unearthly figure. This so terrified the young woman that she screamed and ran for the nearest house. The occupants found her pale and shaking, and several men went out to look for the 'ghost', but nothing was found.

Later the same evening in Muirton Road, Lochee, a young man heard a woman's cry behind him. He turned and saw a weird figure all in white striking a menacing pose in front of the young woman who had just screamed. The 'ghost' then ran away while the man ran home and brought his collie and his terrier to the scene to hunt the figure down, but by that time it had completely vanished.

Although the newspaper report in the *Dundee Evening Post* doesn't give names of the various witnesses, it suggests that they were from the large Irish community. The paper commented that the population was so angry at the ghostly pranks that preparations were being made for a 'Donnybrook', a reference to a notoriously riotous Irish fair, and that the young lads were preparing to meet the ghost with their shillelaghs (a large walking stick or club, with a threatening knob on the end) in hand.[3]

Over the next few nights in late December, the ghost's antics continued. A strong young ploughboy was walking home through the lanes whistling to ease his nervousness. Looking out over a turnip field, he was horrified to see the strange white figure performing 'insane antics'. The shock, we are told, nearly sent him into fits, and he ran home as the ghost disappeared back into the turnip field. Several women who had encountered the ghost had gone into 'acute hysterics', and many were afraid to leave their homes in the hours of darkness. A policeman came across the ghost in a field, gave chase, but could not catch it. Some sources say it was the ghost who chased the policeman. In any case, the locals formed search parties and, clutching their cudgels, went on nocturnal ghost hunts.[4]

It was at this time that the newspaper reports started to refer to the ghost as 'Spring-heeled', though up to this point the accounts had said little about what the ghost looked like. The reports only described a figure in white and made no mention of it having springs on its heels. 'Spring-heeled' was, of course, a reference to the folkloric figure of Spring-Heeled Jack, the demonic trickster who could leap impossible heights, supposedly through having springs on his boots, and who would scare, scratch, or vomit fire in the faces of his victims in Victorian London and beyond well into the twentieth century. It's not at all clear if Jack was a daring hoaxer, or several hoaxers working independently or a result of the overactive imagination of the victims or even whether some of the victims had invented the attacks. Possibly all of the above were true. In any case, Jack became so iconic that any ghost hoaxer might be referred to as a 'Spring-Heeled Jack', and the name was soon attached to the Lochee Ghost in the December of 1900.

That the people of Lochee were on edge is clear from the various false alarms that occurred as Christmas drew near…

Advert for a Spring-Heeled Jack penny dreadful, 1886

The Copper's Tale

A policeman on night duty in late December in a lonely part of Dundee was patrolling an area of parkland as midnight struck. Looking across the park, he observed an eerie white figure moving in the darkness. Thinking he had found the person responsible for the ghost scares, the policeman hid his lantern behind his back so that he could not be easily seen and crept towards the mysteriously moving white object.

As he drew nearer, he was unnerved to hear the pale moonlit phantom recite phrases from a burial service in cold, sepulchral tones. It was at this moment that the copper pulled his lamp from behind his back and raised it above his head to see – a woman in a white nightdress. The policeman had no doubt expected the white figure to be a young lad pretending to be a ghost for a lark, yet instead was greeted by a wild haired woman in a state of undress reciting a funeral service. This is how the *Dundee Evening Post* described the encounter:

> There she stood, her flowing locks floating on the breeze, clad in a white nightdress, pronouncing something in the form of a benediction, and apparently oblivious to the presence of the man of law and order.[5]

The policeman asked the woman what she was doing, but she became even more agitated and began rushing backwards and forwards, gesticulating madly and speaking incoherently. As he tried to escort her back to the police station, the woman became frantic with terror and screamed for her life, yet the resolute policeman still attempted to take her to the station. However, they were soon stopped by a man who came running from a nearby house. The man told the constable that the woman was suffering from 'nervousness' and begged to be allowed to take her back home. The officer, after assuring himself that the man's account was true, allowed them to return home.

Brannigan's Tale

Another episode reported in the local press involved a young baker's boy referred to as Brannigan, though this is not his real name. The boy was sent on an errand for his employer and had to carry a heavy basket of goods down a dark gloomy road with only the dim glow of his small lantern to light the way. It was a miserable, drizzly night – driech, as they say in Scotland – and Brannigan tried to steady his nerves by whistling 'The Lass of Killiecrankie', a saucy Scottish musical hall song, but this probably only made the darkened road seem more eerie.

Coming along the road in the opposite direction was a young farmhand who, because of the weather, was holding an empty sack over his head like a long cloak. The baker's boy and the farm boy encountered each other in the narrowest part of the path, and as Brannigan held his lantern up he was terrified to see a strange figure with arms aloft wearing some strange kind of cloak. Brannigan froze with terror, and the farm boy, after his initial surprise, realised that Brannigan had mistaken him for a ghost. 'Boo!' he cried, and Brannigan dropped his basket and lantern and ran screaming into the night...[6]

Spring-Heeled Jack

Despite these false alarms, reports of a mysterious figure in white continued to be made and soon spread into nearby areas. In the nearby suburb of Downfield, several ladies were walking home along Pitemton Road on Sunday 16 December when from behind a hedge an apparition suddenly emerged. The ladies shrieked and fled and had to be escorted home. They could give no more account of the ghost's appearance other than it being dressed in white.[7]

However, strange new details about the ghost would soon come to light. An unnamed female factory worker aged twenty was walking along Perrie Street, Lochee on a domestic errand late one night when she came face to face with the apparition.

This is how the *Dundee Evening Post* described the sight that confronted her that evening:

> In front of her stood an awful vision dressed in white... His hat was ablaze with light, and, as the breeze blew the folds of his garments aside, it disclosed vestments of flaming red.[8]

Terrified at this uncanny sight, the woman took to her heels and ran to a nearby friend's house.

Other similar sightings occurred over the next few days. The descriptions were all of a strange figure wearing a long white robe that flapped in the wind revealing a bright red garment underneath, and sporting a blazing hat. It narrowly escaped capture when it was seen cavorting in a field near the Downfield tennis courts. A group of volunteers armed with sticks and bludgeons gave chase to a figure described as 'phosphorescent', but the ghost was too swift and vanished among the trees of Camperdown Woods.

Another witness was a nameless elderly gentleman, described as being a quiet and honest man. He was walking home along Perrie Street when someone leapt out in front of him from a doorway. The 'ghost' was dressed in white and bounced up and down (the only allusion to having springs on his heels in the reports) before striking a dramatic pose. The figure then 'proceeded to ejaculate in a wonderful and terrible way', though we are not told what it said. The 'ghost' then vanished into the night leaving the elderly gentleman in a state of shocked confusion.[9] There was speculation that a youthful prankster was at work, which was reasonable given the fact that 'playing the ghost' was exceedingly common in the late nineteenth and early twentieth centuries.[10] It frequently led to ghost hunting vigilante mobs that often had a carnivalesque atmosphere with men sometimes dressing as women hoping to lure the ghost into making an appearance in order to catch him. This had happened in Lochee itself a few years previously.[11] It also seems likely that the ghost hunters over the Christmas period of 1900, given it was the festive season, may have imbibed a little something to keep them warm on those cold Scottish nights.

Whoever or whatever the ghost was, it was proving very elusive. The press described the various encounters as a 'reign of terror', especially among the more 'timid' members of the community.[12]

In the few days before Christmas, the streets were empty – 'as deserted as the Sahara' as the *Dundee Evening Post* put it. The only people likely to be out on the streets after dark were patrolling police or ghost hunting vigilantes.[13]

The ghost's antics were also affecting the young lovers of Lochee. Finding a secluded spot to bill and coo was increasingly troublesome. Courting couples had to contend with the possibility that their lovers' tryst would be disturbed by ghost hunters, the extra police put on duty to catch the hoaxer, or even the Lochee Ghost himself. And fear can play funny tricks on the mind…

Lovers' Tales

Two young lovers glad to find some time alone sat by the pond at Stobswell Park chatting about the Lochee Ghost and his antics. As they shared scary stories, the young man suddenly stopped talking. He thought he could see a strange white form in the distance. Not wanting to scare his sweetheart, he assumed his eyes were deceiving him and he changed the subject to more romantic matters.

However, the young woman looked around and she too saw the strange figure. 'Look at that,' she whispered as she clung to her companion's arm. The pale figure was rapidly drawing closer and closer. The young man resolved to take on the ghost if it offered him any provocation, and the couple stood their ground as the spectre drew nearer. Although the figure was pale, curiously, there was no blazing phosphorescence as had been seen in other encounters.

Closer, closer... and then it flitted past the couple without even noticing them. Three yards behind this figure was another pale form which also emerged rapidly from the gloom and flew past, again, without heeding them. Then came another, and another... The couple realised they had just witnessed the local cross country running club's evening training session.[14]

However, the press speculated that police patrols in Lochee had forced the ghost into nearby areas, as another courting couple were to find out on 21 December. At 9pm in the evening, two young sweethearts were sitting on a bench overlooking High Common in nearby Arbroath. The young woman chanced to look round and saw the head of a man peering at her over a wall. She screamed and set off running. Her puzzled boyfriend ran after her and, looking back, saw a tall figure in white waving its arms in the air. The couple ran as fast as they could to the village and told the people they met what they had seen.[15]

This was clearly a hard time for young love in Lochee. The *Dundee Evening Post* even went on to claim that because young couples were afraid to go courting there was an increase in marriages as that was the only way they could find the opportunity to be alone together.[16]

The Milkman's Tale

Over Christmas, the ghost seemed to have left Lochee for surrounding areas such as the nearby suburb of Broughty Ferry. Shortly before Christmas, a milkman was doing his rounds in the early hours of the morning. As he passed the gloomy remains of Claypotts Castle he saw a figure emerge from the shadows and run out into the middle of the road. The apparition was wearing a fawn coloured cloak with a white sheet around his body and a light coloured tile hat.

Claypotts Castle, Dundee (Gunther Tschuch)

More sightings of the strange white figure with the blazing phosphorescent hat occurred on Christmas Day, though again the volunteers could not catch the culprit.[17]

After Boxing Day, the ghostly visitations stopped as suddenly as they had started.

The Dog's Tale

In the September of the following year, a correspondent for the *Dundee Evening Post* offered a possible explanation for the ceasing of the ghost's shenanigans. A young man named Lona was a dog lover and thought to try his prize terrier as a canine ghost hunter. Over the Christmas period, it's not clear exactly when, Lona, a friend, and Nettle the terrier staged a series of ghost hunts. On the first two nights, they found nothing, but on the third they encountered the mysterious white figure, though on this occasion he was too fast for his pursuers.

The following night Lona and Nettle came across the ghost again in Broughty Ferry, and a frantic chase ensued. Lona warned the fleeing ghost that he would let the dog off the lead if he did not stop, but instead the ghost quickened his pace. 'Take him!' Lona cried, and little Nettle flew after the figure barking furiously and snapping at his flowing white robe.

For once, the ghost was not fast enough and Nettle sunk his teeth into the ghost's all too fleshy leg and refused to let go. Lona caught up and, on unmasking the ghost, was shocked to recognise the culprit as a close friend of his...

Honourably, Lona refused to reveal the name of the friend, presumably extracting from him a promise to cease his nocturnal haunting. If true (and it has to be said, none of the reports of the Lochee Ghost's victims reveal any full names), this would be a good reason for the hoaxer to put a stop to his ghostly activities. Perhaps Nettle, like a wee Scooby Doo, had solved the mystery of Spring-Heeled Jack.

Epilogue

In early September of 1902, ghosts returned to the streets of Lochee with unfortunate consequences. A rumour quickly spread in the Dens Brae part of Dundee that a 'ghost' had scared two little girls to the extent that one of them had fainted and the other had to be carried home. Within minutes, people were hurrying out of their houses forming a mob and shouting 'Where's the ghost? Where's the ghost?' The area was described in the press as being 'wild with alarm'.

As the crowd swelled, a man was seen running down the street and the crowd assumed he was the culprit. They tore after him, and he in turn took fright at the angry mob chasing him and ran into Todburn Lane in the hope of shaking off his pursuers. This was unsuccessful, and the mob crowded round him and dragged him from his hiding place. One of the girls that had been scared by the ghost confirmed that the man was in fact the one who had scared her, leading to the assembled crowd viciously raining kicks and punches on the man, as well as throwing him repeatedly against a wall and battering him violently around the head and face.

Fortunately for the man, a young woman appeared at just the right moment and told the aggressors that they were attacking the wrong man. The crowd left the seriously wounded man to limp home as best he could. The man who was attacked was actually an insurance agent who had been collecting premiums and, as he was behind time, had set off at a run to his final client's house, only to find himself pursued by an angry mob. He was lucky to escape with his life. Two brothers, James and William Wardle along with their mother Mrs Wardle and another woman Mrs Scott, were charged with assault, though only the two men were found guilty and given a fine of seven shillings and sixpence or five days in prison.[18]

There was clearly a great deal of anger among this community of Irish immigrants – or 'Irelands' as they were sometimes called. Perhaps some of this was a leftover from the exploits of the Lochee Ghost that had haunted their streets two years earlier, or perhaps the pressures, hardships, and anxieties of their life as immigrant workers contributed to their resentment and the violent outburst directed at an innocent man. In any case, it would be a brave or a foolhardy individual who would again try and impersonate a ghost…

A few nights later, sixteen-year-old Mary Kennedy was returning home along Wilson Street, Lochee after buying some sweets from the local shop. As she passed a field, she heard a young man, Robert Dundas, a millworker, shout 'Look out, there's a ghost back there!' Mary assumed he was joking and retorted that she was not afraid of ghosts. However, it was then she saw a figure in white on the green that was moving in an eerie manner, coming closer and closer towards her…

Mary screamed and lost consciousness and the next thing she was aware of was lying on the footpath with someone bathing her forehead. She then fainted again and was still unwell the next day.

Robert Dundas was charged with disorderly conduct at Dundee police court on 16 September. He had created his 'ghost' by putting two fish boxes on top of one another with a stone on top and covering the whole with newspaper, shaping it so that it looked like a ghost. Mary Kennedy's febrile imagination did the rest. Dundas said he was sorry for what happened and had only meant it as a joke. Fortunately for him, his good character meant that he escaped prosecution.[19]

Chapter Six

The Violet Farm Poltergeist

'Only the other morning, a big knife whizzed within half an inch of my ear. It has driven my wife away, with the children. They couldn't stand it any longer. Why, only the Sunday before they left, the dinner things flew off the table at them.'

(James Laybourne, 1902)

Over the Christmas of 1902, a Yorkshire farmhouse in Brierley near Barnsley gained a remarkable reputation. It was said to be haunted by a mischievous ghost that mysteriously transported household appliances from room to room, driving the occupants to distraction. Worse than that, the ghost could get violent, throwing rolling pins and knives, and it was even feared that it had pyromaniac proclivities. Word of the haunting spread and the festive season saw ghost hunters, curiosity seekers and journalists drawn to the farm, eventually involving the police and the courts...

The Farmer's Tale

Farmer James Laybourne was a respected and well-known member of his community and had lived most of his life in the South Yorkshire village of Brierley. In 1893 he moved to Violet Farm, an imposing and rather isolated farmhouse surrounded by a kitchen garden, an orchard, and grasslands and there he worked as a tenant farmer with his wife Alice and two children, Alice (eleven) and James, a sickly young man of eighteen. It wasn't long after they moved in that strange events began to occur, culminating at Christmas 1902.[1]

Violet Farm in 1906 (photo unknown)

One day Mrs Laybourne left some dirty laundry to soak in their dolly tub, a barrel-shaped washing tub. Soon after, her husband noticed soap suds seeping under the door. He opened the door to the washroom to see the dolly tub on its side. Bewildered as to how this sturdy washtub could tip over when there was not a soul in the room, he nevertheless stood it up again and put the clothes back in the tub. He left the room and locked it, keeping an eye on the door to make sure nobody entered. After some time, he opened the door again to see the dolly tub upside down with the clothes under it. Some press accounts referred to the house as 'the farm where the dolly tubs danced.'[2]

A dolly tub. The press called Violet Farm 'the farm where the dolly tubs danced'

The mysterious antics of the washing tub were only a part of the strange occurrences that plagued the family. Household items would vanish from one room only to be found later in another. Cushions would fly through the air without warning, as would more dangerous objects like rolling pins, stools, and knives, sometimes apparently aimed deliberately at members of the family.[3] Mr Laybourne told the *Barnsley Chronicle* 'Well, it [the 'ghost'] will hit you with stools and baskets and anything. Things will fly into the fire – cushions and things like that.' The chaos was such that Laybourne said that the ghost had 'played skittles' with every object in the house.[4] Indeed, Mr Laybourne showed visitors to the house scattered debris at the foot of the stairs – burst boxes of starch, books, vegetables, bread, and other items – that had supposedly been flung there by the mischievous ghost.[5]

Strangely, the poltergeist never threw anything at Mr Laybourne until his back was turned. Whenever he looked in the direction he thought a missile had originated from, nothing happened. As soon as his back was turned again, something would be thrown at him. Sometimes he was driven from a room by flying objects, in which case he had learned to walk backwards so that he could avoid being hit. The ghost seems to have particularly taken against Mrs Laybourne, targeting her with rolling pins and other objects, but was also 'cruel' to their young daughter.[6]

The family were not the only witnesses to the mysterious flying objects. The farm's gamekeeper visited Violet Farm to see what was happening. While he was in the kitchen a chair fell over four times in quick succession and cans mysteriously fell off the shelf. The gamekeeper had never been so astounded in his life, and when he left he was 'as pale as death itself'.[7]

One worrying aspect of the apparent haunting was the ghost's predilection for fire. On one occasion, James, the sickly son of the Laybournes, was lying on a bed Mrs Laybourne had made up near the fire – his ill health meant that there always had to be a fire in the room he was resting in. When Mrs Laybourne turned away for a moment, the sick bed moved from its corner and onto the fender near the fire. Books, blankets, pillows, and cushions had also mysteriously found their way up the chimney or onto the fire itself. Mr Laybourne found all this worrying as not long before the strange events began to happen, some of the farmer's outhouses had burned down mysteriously. The worry was such that Mr Laybourne felt that he could not sleep, telling the *Manchester Courier*: 'Owing to the ghost's conduct, I had to remain up for five days and nights for fear it would set the house on fire.'[8]

Mr and Mrs Laybourne were at a loss for what to do. Mr Laybourne was convinced that their house was haunted, as he told the press: 'It is haunted with something we cannot see; it is an unseen thing. I think I shall see what the Spiritualists have to say about it.'[9] Indeed, as word of the missile-throwing pyromaniac poltergeist spread through the surrounding area, the Spiritualists offered some advice: 'Don't fight it, whatever you do, but talk to it, always talk to it, you'll be alright.'

This was perhaps good advice, given Mr Laybourne's state of mind. On one occasion he took his shotgun with the intention of shooting the ghost. How one would shoot an invisible ghost is unclear, though perhaps he planned to wheel around and fire at wherever he thought the missile had come from. More to the point is how one could shoot an invisible spirit that was presumably already dead. Laybourne told the newspapers: 'One day, I thought I would shoot it, but I dare not; that kind of thing makes such a commotion. But what is one to do?'[10]

These were trying times for the family. As well as the ghost's pranks and violent missile hurling and the concern about its obsession with throwing things into the fire or up the chimney, the Laybournes had another problem – ghost hunters. Crowds of curious villagers from Brierley and further afield would hang around outside the farm hoping to catch a glimpse of some ghostly action, or at least to share gossip about the haunting. These amateur ghost hunters would also climb over walls and fences to wander around the farm hoping to see something paranormal. A Christmas ghost hunt would also be the ideal time to imbibe some Christmas spirit and scare one other with spooky stories at a supposedly haunted location, an activity modern folklorists sometimes called 'legend tripping'. However, Mr Laybourne was not at all happy, and after some damage to his property he complained to the police who agreed to keep a watch for trespassers.[11]

Finally, it became too much for Mrs Laybourne and on 20th December she took little Alice and poor ailing James and moved in with the Laybourne's grown up son in a nearby farm.[12] The final straw had come when the ghost turned more and more dangerous, as Mr Laybourne told the press:

> Only the other morning, a big knife whizzed within half an inch of my ear. It has driven my wife away, with the children. They couldn't stand it any longer. Why, only the Sunday before they left, the dinner things flew off the table at them. For at least two days before she left the farm she daren't leave her room.[13]

Mr Laybourne and his farm hand Fred Snowden were now alone in Violet Farm. They would soon be visited by a rather different presence...

The Miners' Tale

Among the many who paid clandestine visits to Violet Farm hoping to see some ghostly activity were four miners from the nearby pit village of Grimethorpe. On the evening of Sunday 21 December, the day after Mrs Laybourne and the children had been chased from the house, James Turner, John Scott, Benjamin Thompson, and James McQueen made their way to Brierley under cover of darkness to see what all the fuss was about.

Christmas is an ideal time for a ghost hunt, and even if the miners did not really believe in ghosts, they steeled themselves with some Dutch courage as they planned to break into the haunted farmhouse and wait there until midnight in order to see what happened. They had heard rumours about the ghost, and it was said in the village that nobody dared stay in the farmhouse after midnight for fear of meeting it, but these intrepid four were made of sterner stuff.

They crept up to the farm looking for a way to get in. Two of the men entered the farmhouse through a window they had broken. Drunken ghost hunting is hungry work, so on entering the kitchen these two set to eating Mr Laybourne's supper and quickly polished off two chops and a cutlet. The other two miners were still outside, perhaps struggling to summon the courage to enter the haunted building, and just as they were about to climb through the window a heavy hand was felt upon their collars. It was the police who had been watching the men for some time after complaints by Mr Laybourne about trespassing ghost hunters and the damage they were doing. Inside, of course, the police also apprehended the other two miners as they were just finishing off Mr Laybourne's supper.

The four men, who were described as 'the worst for drink', were charged with being 'on enclosed premises', a charge used when there was no evidence of attempted burglary. John Scott told the court: 'I don't believe in ghosts and I went to stay on until 12 o'clock, but instead of the ghost it was a constable who came.' At this statement, the court dissolved into laughter, and the drunken ghost hunters were each fined forty shillings plus costs.[14]

The Journalist's Tale

As Christmas rolled into New Year 1903, interest in the ghost did not die down, at least partly because the antics of the drunken ghost hunting miners were widely reported. On 2 January an unnamed reporter from the *Sheffield Evening Telegraph* visited Violet Farm to see what had happened since Mrs Laybourne and the children had moved out.

As the reporter approached the farm, he found an eerie silence and no sign of life except for a few birds. As he walked around, he heard the sound of digging and followed it until he came to Mr Laybourne who was busy shovelling coal. The reporter asked the farmer about the ghost, to which Mr Laybourne replied: 'You'll only call me a liar if I tell you anything. I shall tell you naught.'

However, Mr Laybourne's attitude soon softened and he confirmed that since his wife and children had gone, there had been no repetition of the ghostly activity, though his family were due to return later that day. 'It's only at my wife and the little girl that these things are thrown,' he told the journalist, contradicting most of the earlier reports. 'They've never come at me, so we shall see if they start again'.

The farmer told the journalist that he had also been visited by four Spiritualists who wanted to investigate. Mr Laybourne was reluctant to let them in, but as one had come all the way from Huddersfield, he relented and let them look around the house. It's not clear what the Spiritualists discovered, though when they left they said they had found all they could without the farmer's wife and daughter being present.

When asked what could explain the mysterious events, Mr Laybourne told the journalist that he had a theory. He believed that lightening must have struck the farm's lightening conductor at some time and had electrified the house. This had allowed a spirit from the great beyond, one presumes, to make its presence felt in our world in a way analogous to the way telegraph wires could carry messages. Another suggestion was that the farmhouse may have been built on the site of an old abandoned mine and that the ghostly activity was somehow related to this.[15]

As far as we know, though, the Laybournes were left in peace and the Christmas poltergeist ceased its activity.

Epilogue

Of course, if you want a more down to earth explanation of the Violet Farm Poltergeist that doesn't rely on dubious notions of electrification and haunted abandoned mines, then you need look no further than the Laybournes' sickly young son, James. Although apparently in poor health, he may well have had a mischievous streak. The evidence against him is somewhat circumstantial, though it is still rather compelling. As he was in poor health, the family was obliged to always have a fire going in whatever room he was in, making it easy for him to surreptitiously throw things into the fire or stuff them up the chimney. It may also be noted that all the missiles were thrown at Mrs Laybourne and her daughter (and perhaps Mr Laybourne, assuming the earlier reports are correct), but the ghost never troubled the young boy. Few would suspect a poor young invalid of such trickery…

In any case, you can't keep a good ghost down for long, and a couple of weeks later the ghost was back, though this time it was rumoured that the spook had moved to the village of Havercroft. *The Barnsley Chronicle* reported that many villagers were now afraid to go out at night without being accompanied by friends or the protection of a stout cudgel…[16]

A poltergeist pictured in *La Vie Mysterieuse* magazine, 1911

Chapter Seven

The Calverley Ghost ~ A Yorkshire Tragedy

'Old Calverley, Old Calverley, I have thee by th' ears
I'll cut thee in collops unless thou appears...'
(Chant to raise the spirit of executed child killer, Walter Calverley)

The West Yorkshire village of Calverley became the centre of public attention at Christmas 1904 after reports of a mysterious phantom were widely published. However, the Christmas ghost of Calverley has a long history, involving tales of schoolboys raising the dead, headless horses, exorcism, and haunted preachers. The story begins, though, with a horrifying Jacobean murder spree that spawned a grim piece of gory theatre that William Shakespeare may have had a hand in...

Prologue ~ A Yorkshire Tragedy

In the West Yorkshire village of Calverley, between Leeds and Bradford, stands Calverley Old Hall, once the family home of the illustrious Yorkshire family who gave their name to the village and the ancient house. It was in the oak-panelled bedroom of this house that Walter Calverley committed his infamous murders in 1605.

Much of what we know about the Calverley murders comes from an anonymous pamphlet published in 1605 titled *Master Calverley's Unnatural and Bloody Murder*. The pamphlet also formed the basis for a Jacobean domestic drama called *A Yorkshire Tragedy* (1608) which was once attributed to William Shakespeare, though modern scholars consider Shakespeare's contemporary Thomas Middleton to be the true author.[1] In any case, the gory drama is perhaps the Jacobean equivalent of a sensational modern serial killer docudrama or true crime show.

The account below is based on the 1605 pamphlet and the play. Some may find it upsetting.

Walter Calverley was one of Yorkshire's most eligible bachelors in his youth. He was to inherit a substantial fortune from his deceased parents and had been lovingly taken care of by a notable gentleman who mysteriously remains anonymous in the sources. Walter courted a young woman, the daughter of a local worthy, and the young couple were betrothed to marry once Walter came of age. However, the youth soon forgot his first love and instead married Philippa Brooke, the niece by marriage of the honourable gentleman who had raised him. On hearing of his betrayal, his first love suffered from such great sorrow that she fell ill with consumption and came near to death. She had, in fact, had a lucky escape. Local legend has it that Calverley's callous treatment of his abandoned love led to a curse upon him.[2]

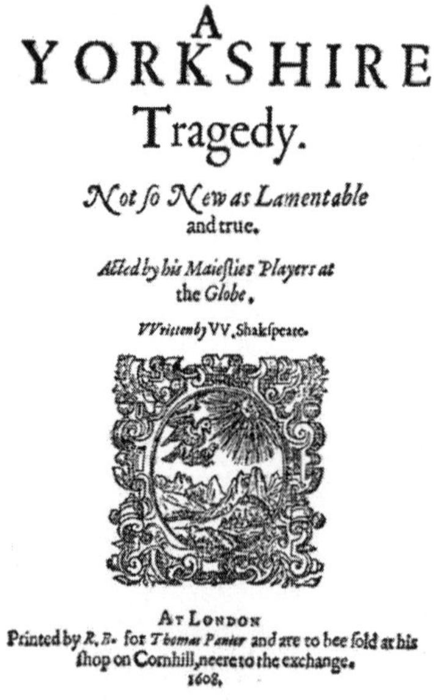
A YORKSHIRE
Tragedy.

Not ſo New as Lamentable
and true.

Acted by his Maieſties Players at
the *Globe*.

VVritten by VV. Shakſpeare.

AT LONDON
Printed by *R. B.* for *Thomas Pauier* and are to bee ſold at his
ſhop on Cornhill, neere to the exchange.
1608.

Title page of the quarto publication of *A Yorkshire Tragedy*, 1608 falsely attributed to Shakespeare

As the years passed, Walter Calverley's disposition altered as he became more and more addicted to various vices. His excesses were such that he frittered away his fortune on (as the play puts it) 'Dice, and voluptuous meetings, midnight revels'.[3] With his fortune all but gone, to maintain his lavish lifestyle he mortgaged his lands and fell further and further into debt. Some of his debts were taken out using his friends and even his brother as bonds on the loans. Should he fail to repay the loans, they could be taken into debtor's prison. As his debts spiralled, Calverley fell into despair and took to walking the grounds of his estate in sullen, resentful desolation. If his wife Philippa enquired what the matter was, Calverley would ignore or insult her, saying 'a plague upon thee, thou art the cause of my sadness.'

To try and salvage his finances, in the spring of 1605 Calverley instructed his wife to go to her uncle in London and arrange for the sale of the lands that had been her dowry. She meekly agreed. However, that honourable gentleman knew of Calverley's excessive habits and profligate ways, and thought they were just youthful excess. Rather than sell her dowry, her uncle said he would arrange for Walter to have a position in the court of King James. Philippa was overjoyed at this. Their financial troubles would be over and her husband would be moving in elevated circles. She thought her desperate husband would be glad of these tidings. She was wrong.

Calverley Hall in 2016 (Mark Stevenson)

With his wife away in London, Calverley's vices became even more excessive than before as he revelled in drink, gambling, and 'other things' until the last of his money and his credit ran out. When he was no longer able to indulge as before, resentment began to fester and a loathing for his wife and children grew within him. In the play, Calverley puts it like this:

> I hate the very hour I chose a wife.
> A true trouble, three children like three evils
> Hang upon me. Fie, fie, fie!
> Strumpet and bastards, strumpet and bastards![4]

Calverley would frequently refer to his wife and children in these insulting terms in public, and while his wife was still away this nearly led to his death. When an anonymous gentleman reproved Calverley for insulting his wife and children, a quarrel developed which became even more heated when Calverley insinuated that the gentleman was on intimate terms with Mrs Calverley – that he was her 'private' friend. The gentleman's honour had been besmirched, and this could only be settled with a duel. As their rapiers clashed, Calverley was wounded, but refused to give up. Bleeding profusely from his side, he continued to fight but was soon overcome and disarmed by his foe. However, the gentleman spared Calverley, exhorting him rather to mend his ways. Calverley, though, was convinced that it was his wife that had led to his wound and his humiliation. In the pamphlet, Calverley says ominously 'Strumpet, thou art the cause that I bleed now, but I will be the cause that thou shalt bleed after.'

As the bloodied Calverley arrived home, he found that his wife had returned from her visit to London. He asked her if she had the money from the sale of her lands, and she told him the news about his being given a position at court. Calverley was incandescent with rage, accusing his wife of complaining about him to her uncle and of robbing him of his independence – if he refused to do as he was told at court, he thought he could be forced to give up his land. Furthermore, Calverley thought that his wife had tricked him to save her from having to sell her land. In his fury at being thwarted, Calverley pulled out his dagger, though at this point a servant entered and told him that a gentleman from his brother's university had called to see him.

Calverley left his wife and went to meet his visitor, who was the master of the university college his brother attended. It was not good news. His brother had a glittering academic career ahead of him but was now languishing in debtor's prison. Calverley's brother had been used as bond for one of his loans and, as it had not been paid, the youth found himself liable for it and imprisoned. The university master was told to wait outside for a while and Calverley would resolve the issue to his brother's satisfaction.

Calverley meanwhile wandered the corridors of his grand house brooding on how his lavish and selfish lifestyle had brought ruin upon his brother, and the poverty that was waiting for his wife and children. He sobbed and tore his hair out, and the pamphlet attributes the following anguished lament to him:

> Oh, I am the most wretched man that ever was born of a woman! Oh, that I had been slain in my mother's womb, and my mother had been my sepulchre! I have begot my children to be nothing but wretchedness, made a wife to eat her bread in bitterness, and a brother to be full of care.[5]

At this moment, Calverley's eldest son, four-year-old William entered the room playing with his spinning top and asked his father how he was. Calverley grabbed the boy by the neck and pulled out his dagger. He raised it and twice hesitated before plunging it into William's head, saying 'Tis charity to brain you.' According to the drama, the boy said pitifully 'How shall I learn now my head's broke?'[6] Holding the wounded child at arm's length to avoid getting blood on his clothes, he carried him into the bed chamber where his wife was resting and the nurse was dressing his second son, Walter. On seeing Calverley with the bleeding infant and bloody knife, the nurse tried to protect the boy she was dressing, but Calverley grasped her, dragged her to the top of the high staircase that led off from the bedroom and hurled her down where she lay unconscious.

The cries of the fearfully wounded William woke his mother and she too tried to protect her second child by holding him in her arms as Calverley lunged at him repeatedly with his dagger. Mrs Calverley took some of the stabs directed at the child herself to try and save him, and she only avoided a fatal wound because the whalebone corset she wore deflected some of the blows. She couldn't maintain this, however, and Calverley stabbed his second child in the heart, before delivering several more stab wounds to his wife.

Meanwhile, servants had found the unconscious nurse at the bottom of the stairs and assumed she had fallen. However, at this point William had managed to stagger to the top of the staircase while Calverley was attacking his wife, though suffering from loss of blood, the boy tumbled down the stairs and died. One servant ran up to the bedchamber and witnessing the horror, cried 'O, Sir, what have you done?' Calverley replied, 'That which I repent not of,' and lunged at the servant with his knife. The two struggled desperately, with Calverley using his spurs to slash and tear the servant's body and face before leaving him bleeding and dashing from the room. Calverley had one more child, Henry, who was being taken care of by a wet nurse twelve miles from Calverley Hall.

As he made for the stables, he met the university master in the grounds and told him to go inside for he had resolved his brother's difficulties. Calverley jumped on a horse and fled, though after entering and seeing the carnage, the master raised a hue and cry and gave chase himself. As Calverley approached the cottage where his baby son was being nursed, his horse stumbled and fell, and at last the murderer was captured. As the ground was flat, the suggestion in the pamphlet was that it was divine intervention that made his horse fall and saved his youngest son from his bloodlust.

Calverley was taken before Justices of the Peace Sir John Savile and Sir Thomas Blande where he explained his actions:

> I have done that, Sir, I rejoice at, and repent this, that I had not killed the other. I had brought them to beggary, and am resolved I could not please God better than by freeing them of it.[7]

A Yorkshire Tragedy from an illustrated edition of *The Works of Shakespeare* (Nicholas Rowe)

Calverley also claimed that he had formed the intention of killing his children two years previously, and further that he feared that his wife had intentions on his own life. In any case, Calverley was to be taken to prison in Wakefield temporarily as the plague was raging in York.

On the way to Wakefield, they passed Calverley Hall and the prisoner asked if he could see his wife who, though seriously injured, had survived his attack. When Mrs Calverley was brought before him in a chair, she kissed him lovingly and they embraced one another. At this moment in the play, it is suggested that Calverley's actions were the result of the devil possessing his senses. He exclaims:

> ... Now glides the devil from me,
> Departs at every joint, heaves up my nails.
> Oh, catch him new torments that were ne'er invented;
> Bind him one thousand more, you blessed angels,
> In that pit bottomless; let him not rise
> To make men act unnatural tragedies...[8]

At his trial in York, Calverley refused to plead either guilty or not guilty. If he had pleaded guilty his effects would have all gone to the state, leaving his family penniless. To try and force him to enter a plea, Calverley was sentenced to be pressed to death. This meant that he would be stretched out on his back naked and with ropes around his wrists and ankles which were secured to posts or the wall. In this immobile position, a board was placed over him and weights gradually added to it so that he was slowly crushed. Death in this manner was slow and agonising and could take days. It was known as 'Peine Forte et Dure', based on the Norman French for 'hard and strong prison' and was used from 1275 until 1741 in cases where the prisoner was 'mute of malice', refusing to plead. The death was so slow and agonising that sometimes friends or relatives would climb on the weights so that the prisoner's ribs would collapse and death would ensue quickly.[9] This is indeed what is rumoured to have happened to Calverley. In his agony, Calverley begged one of his servants to sit on his chest and end his ordeal which he did, putting his erstwhile master out of his misery. The hapless servant was himself then tried for murder, sentenced to death, and hanged at York, or so the rumour goes.[10]

In the tragic play, Mrs Calverley (or 'the Wife' – the lead characters are not given names in the drama) prophetically laments:

> Murder has took this chamber with full hands
> And will ne'er out as long as the house stands.[11]

Pressed to death for refusing to plead (1780 edition of the *Malefactor Register*)

She was correct. Local legend says that the bloodstains on the floor of the murder room could never be washed clean, no matter how hard they were scrubbed.[12] The notorious murders committed in Calverley Hall would echo down the centuries, as the tragic events were retold and embellished and local legends developed. In one fanciful version in the *Annual Register* for 1770, the massacre is even greater: Calverley murders his wife by putting a battle-axe through her skull and then forces his children – all seven of them – to leap off the castle battlements to suffocate in the slime filled moat below.[13] Instead of Calverley's horse stumbling and him being captured, this eighteenth century version of the story ends rather differently but no less dramatically, as Calverley, after slaying his wife and seven children, gallops into the night intent on murdering his remaining infant:

> ...the moon on a sudden was darkened, he lost himself in the midst of a thick forest, the thunder of Heaven, which now dunned his ears, seemed to roll against him, and summon him to judgment, and the pale lightning appalling his soul, was, to his frantic imagination, the fire of hell preparing punishment intolerable, and tortures excruciating to millions of ages. He stopped, relented, repented, surrendered, and submitted himself to justice.[14]

This gothic retelling of the Calverley murders notwithstanding, the bare bones of the story as related in the 1605 pamphlet and the *Yorkshire Tragedy* are true. However, work by historians suggests that there may be religious and political factors at play that are not immediately obvious, and furthermore that the story has been spun to protect the powerful. For one thing, as historian Edward Garnett has noted, the Calverley family had a history of catholic sympathies, and this was a time of heightened tension – the Gunpowder Plot took place in the November of the same year as the murders. Furthermore, Phillipa Calverley had close family connections with Sir Robert Cecil who was Secretary of State and Lord High Treasurer during the reigns of Queen Elizabeth I and King James. As well as being one of the most powerful statesmen in the land, Robert Cecil also played a key role in uncovering the catholic plot to blow up parliament and assassinate the King.[15] In the play and the pamphlet, Mrs Calverley's uncle had been able to arrange a prestigious position in court for her husband. This anonymous uncle was Sir Robert Cecil. The Calverley murders would therefore have cut right to the heart of the establishment.

Given this background, certain inconsistencies and inaccuracies arise in both the 1605 pamphlet and the Yorkshire Tragedy drama of 1608. While Mrs Calverley is presented as perfect womanhood personified, Calverley is presented as a whoring, drunken gambler living a riotous life. However, as Garnett notes, the opportunities for such activities in a small Yorkshire village in 1605 were rather limited.[16] Furthermore, the pamphlet and the play make much of Calverley sending his wife to London to her guardian to sell the land that was her dowry yet, in reality, her dowry was held in cash and had already been given to Calverley (and spent). In the play, the main characters are not named. In the dramatis personae they are listed as Husband, Wife, Son, and Master of a College. We know that the first three are the Calverley family, but the 'Master of a College' (who is also anonymous in the pamphlet) is something of a mystery. Interestingly, Sir Robert Cecil was Chancellor of Cambridge University at this time, which raises the possibility that the university master of the drama could in fact be Cecil himself.[17] We will probably never know what murky intrigues were playing out behind the scenes in the Yorkshire Tragedy of 1605, but the involvement of Robert Cecil would certainly mean that the events would be recorded in such a way as to flatter – or at least avoid scandalising – his side of the family.

Robert Cecil, 1st Earl of Salisbury by John De Critz the Elder

There is no doubt, though, that Walter Calverley visited an orgy of destruction on his family on 23 April 1605. Mrs Calverley survived the horrific attacks of her murderous husband and later remarried and had three more children. She died shortly after the birth of her third child in 1613. Calverley's surviving son Henry went on to live in Calverley Hall, where he died in 1652.[18]

A Night in the Murder Room ~ The Preacher's Tale

The village of Calverley shuddered under the early January snow one Saturday evening in the late eighteenth century, let's say 1777.[19] Renowned methodist preacher Richard 'Dickie' Burdsall spent the night in the Murder Room at Calverley Hall, and recorded what happened in his 1797 autobiography, *Memoirs of the Life of Richard Burdsall*. With the murders being over a century in the past, Burdsall had not heard of them when he visited the village.[20]

After a well-received sermon in front of a large congregation in Calverley Hall, Burdsall was taken upstairs to the room where he was to sleep as a guest. On finding himself alone after a long day, he knelt down in the large room with the oak-panelled ceiling and said his prayers before climbing into bed and drifting off to sleep around midnight. This is how he describes what happened next:

> ... and after being asleep some little time, I thought something crept upon me up to my breast, pressing me much; I was greatly agitated and struggled to awake.

Not only was something crawling onto his chest and crushing the life out of him, his bed seemed to swing such that he was thrown upon the floor. He got to his knees and gave thanks that he was unhurt.

He returned to bed still wondering at what had happened and if he had really been thrown out of the bed, or if he had got out himself. After fifteen minutes or so pondering this, he was again flung from the bed and tumbled onto the floor. Alarmed and confused he prayed again, and then lay flat on his stomach and crept under the bed to see if he could see any reason why it might swing or move. He found nothing.

After another prayer he returned to bed once again, questioning his sanity. A third time he found himself thrown onto the floor. He called out for God's help in bewilderment, and again inspected the bed and saw that all four legs were solid and on the floor.

The Murder Room, Calverley Old Hall (from *Loidis and Elmet* by Thomas Dunham Whitaker 1816)

By now it was one in the morning, and Burdsall decided that he would not lie down on the bed again and so he got dressed. On several occasions he went to the bedroom door as if to leave the room, and he was about to cry out and wake the household, but he seems to have ultimately decided to face his waking nightmare alone. At a loss to explain what was happening to him in this gloomy oak-paneled room, he could only conclude that Satan himself was testing his faith. This is how Burdsall described his agonising wait until daybreak:

> I longed to see the light of the morning, and had I been immured in a dungeon and heavily fettered in irons I think I could not have been more desirous of my liberty than I was for the return of the morning.

When the wintry light eventually crept through the window of the oak-panelled bed chamber with the dark stains on the floor, Burdsall saw that his room adjoined the churchyard, and below him, under ancient yew trees were the snow-covered melancholy graves of many past inhabitants of this great Yorkshire hall.

Of course, when Burdsall related his nocturnal adventure to his hosts, they informed him of the Calverley murders of 1605. They would also have told him about Walter Calverley's agonising execution, where he was slowly pressed to death – a demise that seems eerily similar to the preacher's experience of something crushing his chest.

However, if you've ever experienced sleep paralysis, a fairly common sleep disorder, you might recognise elements of Burdsall's night of terror. When sleep paralysis strikes, nightmarish hallucinations often accompany the feeling that someone – or something – is crushing one's chest. These waking nightmares feel utterly real, and being paralysed and unable to escape adds to the terror. Perhaps Burdsall suffered an episode of sleep paralysis, and later interpreted it in the light of the murders that had been committed in the room in which he had slept.

Furthermore, we don't really know whether (or how much) Burdsall embellished his experience. Historian and Calverley resident Edward Garnett points out that Burdsall somewhat spoiled his story by saying his room looked out onto the graveyard. There is no view of the graveyard from Calverley Hall.[21]

It seems likely that The Preacher's tale would have spread quickly through the community, and those of a certain age might remember tales their grandparents told them of 'Owd Calverley' and his monstrous deeds. And so ghostly legends and traditions, and eventually a Christmas connection, began to emerge.

Ghosts of Calverley

If you were riding across Greengates Beck Bottom in Calverley after dark in the early nineteenth century, you might feel someone leap onto the back of your horse, and not leave you until the beck was crossed. This was the ghost of Owd Calverley, according to local legend.

There were also stories that Calverley's ghost would gallop around the village of a night clutching his bloodied dagger on a headless horse. Sometimes he might be accompanied by the faithful servant who had put an end to his master's sufferings and paid with his own life. He too, of course, would be on a headless horse. There seems to be no particular reason why the horses were headless, apart from, perhaps, it creates a striking ghostly image. Some accounts even have the ghost of Owd Calverley himself carrying his head under his arm, even though he was not beheaded.

In any case, as Owd Calverley's ghost atop his headless horse galloped through Calverley woods, it would cry 'A pound more weight – lig on, lig on' – 'lig' being Yorkshire for 'lie'.

This was supposedly what Calverley had said as he was being slowly crushed to death, according to local lore. Of course, if the ghost confined itself to the woods, he wasn't much bother, but he created great consternation if he rode his ghastly horse into the village. Locals say that a skilful exorcist cast a charm that prevented Owd Calverley from passing the church as long as the holly grew green in Calverley Woods.[22] These legends may have been recorded by Rev George Stanley Faber, curate at Calverley between 1803 and 1806. According to Edward Garnett, Faber may also have been the cunning exorcist who finally confined Calverley's restless spirit to the woods and stopped his haunting of the village. The reverend also told of an old man who worked as a clerk for the church who had seen Calverley's spectre with his own eyes, though admittedly this was after a heavy night of 'drinking and carding'.[23]

Although the ghost-busting curate was supposed to have exorcised Calverley's ghost, many of the village children believed that the evil spirit could be raised if you performed a certain ritual. An anonymous correspondent reminisced about his childhood ghost hunts in the *Bradford Observer*.[24] In order to summon Old Calverley's spirit, first the children would pile their caps in a pyramid in the churchyard and some pins and breadcrumbs leftover from tea were scattered about. Then the children would hold hands to form a circle around their caps and recite the magic words:

> Old Calverley, Old Calverley, I have thee by th' ears,
> I'll cut thee in collops unless thou appears.[25]

Collops are cutlets or slices of bacon.

At the same time as the recitation was being chanted, some of the braver boys would go and whistle through the keyhole of the church door before repeating the rhyme. The correspondent claims that on one occasion he and his friends saw – or thought they saw – a pale and ghostly figure appear, though they did not stay to have a proper look but fell over themselves in a mad dash to escape the graveyard.

The ghost of Owd Calverley was also thought to have been responsible for a campanological mystery. Around Christmas 1872 the bell in the church tower at Calverley began tolling in the early hours of the morning. They continued ringing for a long time, and the villagers came running from their warm beds into the cold night to see what the matter was. The door to the church was locked, but still the bells tolled. For a long time, the bells rang on as the villagers searched for the key to the church door which could not be found. When it was finally located, the bells stopped the instant the key was put in the lock.[26]

Perhaps it was the Preacher's winter adventure, or the mysterious tolling of the church bells in December 1872 that first connected Calverley's ghost with Christmas. Or perhaps it's his name being associated with holly that makes him a seasonal ghost, for the exorcist's charm made the murderer's shade avoid the village while the holly trees grew green in Calverley Wood. Or it could just be that everyone loves a ghost story at Christmas.

The Horsforth Man's Tale

In 1904, some boys started a fire that left twenty acres of the holly trees in Calverley Wood burned black. Could this be why the ghost of Old Calverley chose the Christmas of that year to make his presence known again?

On Sunday 18 December 1904, a gentleman referred to only as 'the Horsforth Man' (after a village near Calverley) was walking home past the church yard. It was a cloudy night, though at times pale moonlight peered through the darkness. According to the *Yorkshire Evening Post*, this is what happened next:

> ...without any preliminary warnings there was a flash and a phantom-like form floated before the astonished pedestrian. He was all alone, the villagers having long since retired to bed. The apparition then disappeared, and all was quiet again.[27]

The next day the Horsforth Man told a friend who was acquainted with local folklore about his experience. When he heard about the Yorkshire Tragedy, he became convinced that he had seen the ghost of Owd Calverley himself.[28] Of course, the story was widely reported in the local and national media, and locals once again went on nocturnal ghost hunts in the hope of catching Calverley's restless spirit.[29]

Epilogue

There was some scepticism about the Horsforth Man's story, and the anonymity of the witness suggests the possibility that the story was a journalistic joke, 'trading on the credulity of a number of London journals,' as the *Leeds Mercury* put it.[30] The *Mercury* suggested the mysterious Horsforth Man didn't even exist – and if he did, his spooky experience was a case of one too many down the pub:

> [The Horsforth Man] who, if he exists at all outside the fertile imagination of an enterprising newspaper correspondent, had probably been keeping out the fog and cold at a neighbouring hostelry before he arrived at a sufficiently exalted condition to commune with denizens of another world.

Calverley Hall is now holiday lets.

The *Yorkshire Tragedy* lives on as a gory curio in Shakespeare's apocrypha.

Chapter Eight

The Dronfield Skeleton

> **'It was over in the corner, not far from the door – a hideous, ghastly sight. It was a skeleton, and yet the fleshless bones seemed animated with life. The ugly eye-sockets appeared to see. She could not take her eyes off them. She was held with a speechless terror...'**
>
> ***(Sheffield Daily Telegraph, 1906)***

Christmas 1906. A young couple are plagued with mysterious footsteps and unexplained noises after moving into their new house in Dronfield, Derbyshire. After the woman of the house has a terrifying encounter with a ghostly skeleton, locals speculate it's something to do with the mysterious dried-up well in the cellar of the house...

The House with the Well

Sometime before Christmas 1906, an unnamed young couple from Sheffield moved into their new home in Dronfield, Derbyshire. However, the house had an unusual feature – the cellar had a deep, dark, mysterious hole that had remained uncovered for some unknown reason. When the couple asked their neighbours about it, they were informed that the house was built over a disused well. Every time the wife went into the cellar, she would be overcome with a creepy feeling, so she always kept as far away from the well as possible. She would never go into the cellar after dark.

A few nights before Christmas two little girls, children of some Sheffield friends, were staying over with the couple. The wife slept upstairs with the children, but because none of the other bedrooms had been furnished yet, the husband slept on the sofa in the living room – the room above the cellar. In the middle of the night, the wife was awoken by the sound of footsteps on the stairs. The footsteps creaked across the landing and approached the room that she and the two children were occupying, but then seemed to pass and enter another room. Shortly afterwards, she heard the footsteps leaving the room and returning down the stairs. She decided that it must have been her husband going to get some blankets from one of the bedrooms.

At the same time, the husband was having a difficult night on the sofa. He too heard footsteps on the stairs, though he assumed it was his wife going to get something from the kitchen. When they discussed what they had heard the next day, they quickly realised that the footsteps did not belong to one or the other of them. This must have been unnerving for the young couple. In any case, they concluded that the house contained a restless spirit that was somehow connected to the mysterious dark hole in the cellar.

The footsteps weren't the only eerie happenings in this Dronfield house. One corner of a room above the cellar was frequently disturbed with strange knocking sounds. These were described as slow and muffled, as if someone was inside the wall, weakly attempting to hammer his way out. These noises continued night after night, and the couple were so scared that they could only sleep with the gas light burning.

The Wife's Tale

One night, the wife woke up in a state of alarm to find the gas light they kept burning had been extinguished. She was overwhelmed by a feeling of powerlessness and was certain that she was not alone – there was a malevolent presence in the room with her. Try as she might, she was unable to scream or wake her husband. She was frozen in terror, but after a desperate struggle managed to spring from the bed and grab some matches from the dressing table. The *Sheffield Daily Express* of Christmas Eve 1906 takes up the story:

> As the light of the match illuminated the room she looked round, and there, looking her full in the face, and pointing towards her, was a ghost. Spell-bound she watched it until the match flickered out in her fingers.
>
> It was over in the corner, not far from the door – a hideous, ghastly sight. It was a skeleton, and yet the fleshless bones seemed animated with life. The ugly eye-sockets appeared to see. She could not take her eyes off them. She was held with a speechless terror.[1]

After pointing at the woman, the skeleton turned away as if to leave and the match sputtered out. The woman threw herself onto the bed in a state of hysteria and woke her husband up. He desperately scrambled for the matches and relit the gas lamp as his wife screamed in terror, but they were alone in the room.

They did not sleep in the house again. The story clearly perturbed the community. The *Weekly Dispatch* noted rather condescendingly that the 'simple-minded inhabitants, in their attempt to account for the apparition, gravely fear that the deep, dark well has something to do with it.'[2] If one wanted to concoct a ghost legend, then one could speculate that some unfortunate soul was buried alive in the dark well, or was murdered and thrown into its depths. If one prefers a less Victorian gothic and more Lovecraftian approach, then perhaps the hole in the cellar is a portal to the underworld and the skeleton came to warn us of the return of the Old Gods…

Speculation aside, the story of the Dronfield Christmas Skeleton was reported in many British newspapers over Christmas 1906 though, unfortunately, none of the articles gave a name to the young couple or any detail as to where exactly the house was. Perhaps it was an urban legend picked up by a Sheffield journalist who thought the story was too good to ignore and that it would bring some festive spookiness to the Christmas Eve news. However, perhaps there is a germ of truth to the story. After all, the wife's dreadful experience with the ghastly skeleton reads like a perfect description of sleep paralysis, a relatively common sleep disorder in which the victim awakens to find they cannot move (as seen in the previous chapter). There is frequently the sense of an evil presence and terrifying hallucinations. Often the hallucinations involve an intruder, a ghost, witch, or demonic figure. It's an altered state of consciousness between nightmare and wakefulness and feels utterly real.[3] If there is any truth to the story of the Dronfield Skeleton, I suspect that someone had an experience of sleep paralysis and told their friends and family about it. Soon the story took on a life of its own and was jumped on by the press.

However, one strange aspect of the episode is the appearance of a ghostly skeleton. With its tongue firmly in its cheek, the *Sheffield Daily Telegraph* commented on this unusual aspect of the story:

> It is too generally assumed that ghosts have gone out of fashion. The old skeleton ghost certainly has. It is very rarely heard of these days.
>
> They no longer go about in bare bones. Up-to-date ghosts are always clothed in lovely flowing robes of a soft white silky texture; and they also, nowadays, wear a cheerful, comfortable, companiable countenance which never frightens.[4]

The newspaper had a point. The steady rise of Spiritualism and spirit photography where double exposure was used to fake diaphanous images of ghosts draped in voluminous shrouds or gowns had changed people's expectations of what ghosts should look like. The problem with the ghosts of the Spiritualists, however, is that they just weren't scary; if anything they and their messages were often rather banal. The Dronfield apparition, despite its dubious provenance, is at least scary.

However, when it comes to episodes of sleep paralysis, hallucinations tend to be informed by culture and expectation.[5] In modern times, sufferers may hallucinate aliens around the bed, whereas in times past the horrific visions would have been of witches or demons. The vision of a skeleton seems unusual in this regard. Perhaps, though, skeletons would have been on the mind of many residents of Dronfield due to a sensational local mystery that occurred the previous November.

Death and the Lady (Victorian print)

The Skeleton's Tale

Around a mile from Dronfield lies the village of Unstone. Above Unstone lies the hamlet of Summerley where is situated a farm that in 1906 was called by the locals Ashton's Farm. In November of that year workman Thomas Wills was excavating a trench along the side of the farmhouse to improve drainage when his pick hit something hard. It was a human skull. Other parts of the skeleton were also found. It was reported that the body had a bullet hole in the skull and the legs had been doubled up to allow the corpse to be quickly disposed of in a shallow grave. Of course, in the surrounding Derbyshire villages, the talk was of murder. Some locals remembered that some fifty years prior a woman had gone out one night and was never seen again – perhaps this skeleton with the bullet hole in the skull was her? One of the oldest local residents, Mr Gill (eighty) said that he couldn't remember any mysterious disappearances happening in his lifetime, but his father told him that a murderer had cut off a woman's head at nearby Ramshaw Wood. The killer was hanged and publicly gibbeted. Could the skeleton be that of the murderer, or perhaps his victim?

The rumours, though, were rather far from the mark. The skeleton was examined by the police and Dr Rooth, who confirmed that it was female, about five feet, four inches and of 'robust' build. However, there was no bullet hole in the skull; the damage had been caused by the workman's pick. Nor had the corpse been doubled up, though it had been buried at an oblique angle to the west side of the house at a depth of around two feet. The skull had no teeth, and neither were there any clothes nor sign of a coffin. Dr Rooth said the bones were probably 200 years old and were likely to be the remains of a person infected with plague or other infectious disease who was buried rapidly.[6]

As Christmas approached the people of Unstone and Dronfield would have shared gossip, rumours and speculation about the mystery skeleton found at Ashton Farm. Perhaps these bones and the dark stories of murder inspired the anonymous woman's nocturnal vision of a ghostly pointing skeleton.

Epilogue

It's a shame that there are no names given in the Dronfield Skeleton story, so all we have is speculation. My guess is that a couple of a nervous disposition really did have some scary experiences. The mystery footsteps, though, may have been caused by one of the little girls they had staying with them getting up to some mischief. The nervous couple afterwards construed every nighttime creak or bump as a wandering spirit, and lurid tales of murder and skeletal remains primed the wife to have the horrific vision of the skeleton when she was gripped by an attack of sleep paralysis.

It is also entirely possible that some, or all, of the Dronfield Skeleton story was simply a tall tale picked up (or made up) and expanded upon by a journalist for a touch of festive horror.

Chapter Nine

The Ghost of King Richard III on New Year's Eve

'I am King Richard the Third, permitted to visit your miserable earth but once every year. And every New Year's Eve it pleases me to visit the scene where traitors brought about my mortal overthrow... Here I come to fight my last battle o'er again and to wreak shadowy vengeance on the villains that betrayed me. For six brief hours every year I have haunted this spot for the past five hundred years and never before have I condescended to speak to a mortal. To thee I would give a message...'

(King Richard III's Ghost, 1921)

On New Year's Eve 1921 a farmer encountered the luminous green ghost of King Richard III at the site of his final battle. The colourful tale caused a sensation in the national press, and disquiet among the villagers as more rumours of King Dick's wandering ghost spread. Journalists, ghost hunters, and psychic investigators duly followed... But not only did King Dick's ghost have a message to give to the world, he also hid a secret...

The King's Tale

It is 21 August 1485, the night before the Battle of Bosworth – the final act in the Wars of the Roses. King Richard is alone and despondent in his tent on Ambion Hill, west Leicestershire. He drinks some wine and drifts off to sleep. He's then visited by a procession of ghosts – all the men, women, and children whom he had killed to achieve and maintain the crown of England. One by one the ghosts appear: Edward Prince of Wales, King Henry VI, George Duke of Clarence, Lady Anne, Hastings, Rivers, Grey, Vaughan, Buckingham, and the young princes famously murdered in the Tower of London, Edward and Richard. Each ghost curses Richard, telling him one after the other to despair and die.

This is how Shakespeare envisions King Richard's last night, anyway. When Richard wakes from his slumber, he says:

> The lights burn blue; it is now dead night.
> Cold fearful drops stand on my trembling flesh...[1]

The lights burning blue possibly allude to the ghostlore of centuries past when it was thought that the candle burning blue signified the presence of a spirit. Ghosts were often thought to take the form of luminescent blue flames sometimes called corpse candles or death lights. At the moment someone died these bluish flames would leave the house and traverse the path along which the funeral procession was to follow to the church. The corpse candle would then pass into the church where the coffin was to be taken and light up the whole building with brilliant blue light before proceeding to the grave that was soon to be the deceased's final resting place.[2] When the light burns blue, it's as if a portal opens between our world and another. Shakespeare's version of Richard's demise thus begins ominously, but even in historical accounts the omens were not much better.

Richard III and ghosts (William Blake, 1806)

Battle of Bosworth (Philip James de Loutherbourg, 1804)

On the morning of the battle no chaplains could be found in Richard's camp for the divine blessing before battle. This inauspicious start would surely have weighed heavy on Richard and his troops. The King placed his gold crown on his head and mounted his white horse. Some of his supporters advised Richard against wearing the crown, as it would make him an easy target. Richard replied that he would live and die the King of England. However, Richard's army was outnumbered by the combined forces of the rebels led by Henry Tudor, so he gambled on a surprise attack. Richard charged towards Henry, hacking down all who stood in his way and managed to get within yards of his enemy, such was the ferocity of the attack. At some point, though, Richard fell or was knocked from his horse and surrounded by enemy knights. At this point Shakespeare has Richard cry, 'A horse, a horse, my kingdom for a horse!' though contemporary reports say Richard yelled 'Treason!' as the blows rained down on him from all sides.[3] On Ambion Hill, alone and surrounded by enemies, King Richard was beaten about the head and neck with swords and battle-axes until dead. His body was stripped naked and flung over a horse. He received a final insult – a sword wound in the rectum – before being taken to Leicester and rolled into an unmarked grave.[4]

And that was the last anyone saw of Richard for 437 years...

The Farmer's Tale

Bill Chesterton of Tinsel Lane was described rather unkindly by *The Nuneaton Chronicle* as a bluff, burley farmer who was a 'plain matter-of-fact son of the soil, with as much imagination as one of his turnips.'[5] On New Year's Eve 1921 Farmer Chesterton had been drinking with friends at the Dog and Hedgehog where he'd met his mate, Ben Giles. After the obligatory one for the road, the two set off walking home and on the way got into a disagreement about the location of a fox den in the woods on Ambion Hill. They were both hunters, so they decided to settle the matter there and then and traipsed up the hill to the edge of the woods. When they got there, they started to wish they hadn't. The woods were dark and misty, and a howling wind was blowing through the trees, jagged against the pale moonlight. As they entered deeper, an owl flew by and knocked Ben's hat off and, as he bent to pick it up, he fell into a ditch. At this point a green light was seen glowing among the trees, and this was enough for Farmer Giles to take to his heels, but Chesterton was not so easily scared. He approached the light which appeared to be coming from a place near King Richard's Well, a cairn erected in 1813 marking the place where Richard took his final drink, according to local legend.[6]

It was here in this wintery woodland that Chesterton came face to face with the ghost of the long-dead monarch. He later described the ghost as being an ugly, old, hump-backed devil with glowering bloodshot eyes that seemed to look right through him. He was wearing a golden crown and a fur-lined plum-coloured velvet cloak, and he was carrying his sword. Around him was an uncanny luminous green haze that seemed to follow him whenever he moved.[7] As the trembling farmer stood amazed, the ghost commanded his attention: 'Varlet! Listen to me.' His voice was hoarse, according to Chesterton, sounding like a rusty key turning in an old lock. The royal spectre continued:

King Richard's Well on Ambion Hill (Nick Macneill, 2002)

> I am King Richard the Third, permitted to visit your miserable earth but once every year. And every New Year's Eve it pleases me to visit the scene where traitors brought about my mortal overthrow. It was at yonder well I quenched my royal thirst in my last hours of agony. Here I come to fight my last battle o'er again and to wreak shadowy vengeance on the villains that betrayed me. For six brief hours every year I have haunted this spot for the past five hundred years and never before have I condescended to speak to a mortal. To thee I would give a message...[8]

The message King Richard III had for Bill Chesterton was surprisingly environmental. The King was not happy that woodcutters had been felling the trees in the woods on Ambion Hill. 'Tell the woodsmen to stay their hands in future,' Richard said, 'or dire misfortune will dog their footsteps even as surely as it dogged mine on that sultry August day of long ago.' Bill promised to deliver the message.

Earliest surviving portrait of Richard III

At this point, the ghost grew somewhat nostalgic and misty eyed, according to Chesterton's account. The King gazed over the sight of his final struggle. 'Aye! 'Twas a joyous fight while it lasted,' he said. 'It was a big grave they had to dig at yonder hamlet of Dadlington – two thousand as brave bowmen as ever played with death!' Chesterton replied that the Battle of Bosworth was child's play compared to modern wars, referring to World War One, where deaths are counted not in thousands but in millions. At this, King Richard laughed in such a way that Chesterton's blood froze in his veins. Richard said they were keeping 'a warm place by the fire' in hell for German Emperor William II. 'Till he arrives I have no real rival in Hell's galaxy of first class fiends… Varlet farewell.'

Upon saying this, the spectre vanished and Chesterton was alone in the dark wood. The farmer took to his heels and arrived home in the early hours of New Year's Day.[9]

A Tall Tale

Bill Chesterton's encounter with King Richard was first reported in a column called 'Round the Farms' in the *Nuneaton Chronicle and West Midlands Farmers Gazette* on 6 January 1922. The tone of the tale is tongue-in-cheek and was presumably invented by the author, Albert Francis Cross, who was also the editor of the paper. The ghost of King Richard is almost cartoonish, with its glowering red eyes, hump, and mysterious green glow, not to mention his cod-Shakspearian dialect and swipes at the German Emperor. However, the story was picked up by other papers and told in condensed form which removed the comical touches that had informed readers that the account was a joke. The *Leicester Evening Mail* reported that at midnight on New Year's Eve, two men were walking home on Ambion Hill when the ghost of King Richard III in his gold crown and luminous green cloak rose from the earth. As one of the men fled in terror, the ghost indicated his displeasure at the felling of trees by silently pointing at them, before vanishing into a heap of stones. These stones possibly refer to the cairn marking the location of King Richard's Well. According to the *Leicester Mail*, many an adventurous young man had ventured into the woods at night in order to catch a glimpse of the spectre, and other locals had seen the ghost walking in the country lanes in its distinct green cloak, and that many were seriously perturbed by the ghostly activity.[10]

This condensed version of the encounter with King Dick was widely reported around the country. The *London Daily News* wondered where the ghost of Richard's horse was. It also noted that, if Richard's fearsome reputation as a tyrant is true (and not just Lancastrian propaganda), then it seems unlikely he would be so bothered about some trees.[11] Indeed, as one London wag commented, Shakespeare has no less than eleven ghosts visit Richard in his tent the night before his final battle and all of them say they are going to sit heavy on his soul. With so many ghosts sitting heavy on Richard's soul, it's a wonder his ghost was able to walk at all.[12]

Nevertheless, journalists from around the country filled their column inches with 'Rambling Richard' and his nocturnal protests against the chopping down of trees on Ambion Hill. This apparently so annoyed the author of the original report of Richard's ghost that he sent a journalist to interview Bill Chesterton to try and get to the bottom of the matter. The journalist, writing under the name of Barn Owl, tells us that Chesterton was actually a pseudonym, but he obtained the man's real name and address from the editor and set off through the snow drifts to meet the enigmatic farmer. Chesterton (we are not told his actual name) offered the Barn Owl a drop of the hard stuff after his freezing journey and they discussed the ghost, with the farmer's dog Owd Rattler keeping a malignant eye on the stranger. When asked about King Dick, Chesterton scoffed at newspaper reports of the luminous green cloak and tales of the spirit wandering the country lanes and villages around Bosworth. The cloak was not luminous, Chesterton reiterated, but plum coloured and fur-lined and there was a luminous green haze that surrounded and followed the apparition. Furthermore, the ghost could not have been seen in the villages as it only visited the earth for six hours every New Year's Eve. 'All I know is this,' said Chesterton. 'King Dick spoke to me and I answered him back again.' Any remotely sceptical questioning of the story by the journalist was met by a threatening growl from Owd Rattler. I suspect that 'Barn Owl' was in fact the *Nuneaton Chronicle's* editor, A.F. Cross writing under a pseudonym, and the last sentences of the article make it even clearer that the editor had made up the story of the farmer who saw the ghost of King Richard protesting the deforestation of Ambion Hill:

> In the article written in this journal a fortnight ago the Editor used the phrase: "bluff Bill Chesterton." I wonder if he used the adjective with any special meaning, or merely for alliterative reasons? My readers will draw their own conclusions.[13]

Despite the unsubtle suggestion that the whole story was a 'bluff', at least one psychic investigator made his way to Nuneaton and enquired at the chemist where Ambion Hill was as he was in search of King Richard's ghost. The chemist gave a ribald laugh and told him that King Dick's ghost didn't come from Ambion Hill, it came from the imagination of the *Nuneaton Chronicle's* staff.[14] As this anecdote was published in the *Nuneaton Chronicle* itself, we might take it as another tacit admission that the whole story was indeed a journalist's tall tale.

Epilogue

King Richard III made a spectacular return to the news headlines in September 2012 when his skeleton was found underneath a Leicester car park. The bones, verified by DNA analysis, confirmed the brutal nature of Richard's death and, also, that he had a curvature of the spine that would have meant that one shoulder was higher than the other.[15] It would be an exaggeration, though, to say he had a hump. Richard's remains were taken to Leicester Cathedral and interred there. However, it was not long before his ghost was active again, though this time not on New Year's Eve. In September 2015 medium and 'psychic artist' Christine Hamlett from Cheshire was visiting the cathedral and felt a calming presence, which she took to be the King's. After taking some photos inside the cathedral, she noticed that one of them seemed to show a face which she thought was Richard's peering out from a stone slab. She told the *Daily Mirror*, 'A car park is no place for a King to be buried but there was a peaceful aura around his tomb – it was as if his spirit appreciated being in a fit and proper place.'[16]

View from Ambion Hill (Tony Grist)

Actor Henry Irving as Richard III

Chapter Ten

The Uxbridge Ghost

> **'The ghost fairly put me through it. He bent over me and mesmerised me. I lay there as if paralysed. If you had said anything about ghosts two years ago I would have laughed. Now I don't.'**
>
> **(Bert Burrows, 1922)**

From just before Christmas 1921 to January 1922, Uxbridge was buzzing with rumours of a mysterious ghost. Strange footsteps, mysterious poltergeist activity, and a weird ghostly presence terrified the Burrows family, and several intrepid psychic investigators and mediums tried to solve the mystery of the unquiet spirit. However, there was little agreement as to who the unwelcome visitor actually was…

The Jobmaster's Tale

Mr Gilbert Burrows was a practical man, known for his common sense and in no way in possession of an excitable imagination. He was once a fireman who had driven his horse-drawn fire wagon around early twentieth-century Uxbridge, West London, though his skills were no longer required when motors replaced the horses. As Christmas 1921 approached, Mr Burrows was working as a jobmaster – a stable keeper – and lived on Cowley Road, Uxbridge with his wife, four sons, and daughter. His horses lived in the stable adjoining the back of the house.

But for all his down-to-earth common sense, Mr Burrows was convinced his house was haunted by a white figure in a black cap. Odd noises had been heard in the house since the family moved there fifteen years ago, but in the days before Christmas 1921, all kinds of strange things began to take place. The mysterious presence was usually heralded by a blast of icy air that set the family's hair on end; the chill wind would be accompanied by the sound of chains clanking. This noise was variously described as the sound made by several tin baths clanging together, or the rattle of hail on an iron roof. The family would sometimes hear the unnerving clump of a male figure climbing up the stairs at night, though nobody could be seen.

There was also apparent poltergeist activity, Mr Burrows told the press. Fire irons moved mysteriously and doorknobs from upstairs rooms were found at the bottom of the stairs. Sometimes a family member's mattress would suddenly start shaking, sending the terrifying occupant running from the bedroom.[1]

On one occasion in late December, the family heard a great commotion coming from the stables adjoining the house – something was terrifying the horses. The family hurried to the stable, but no matter how hard they tried to open the door, a mysterious force was holding it shut. When they eventually managed to force the door, the horses were clearly distressed, though there was no sign of anyone – or anything – in the stables. The horses were in such a state of shock that they were unable to work for the next few days, it was reported.[2]

The ghost itself was usually described as being an elderly man dressed in white with a close-fitting black cap or skull cap. Strangely, although some newspaper accounts claim several witnesses had seen the ghost, other reports say the presence was 'felt' rather than seen.[3] Obviously, if the ghost was felt rather than seen, it's unclear where the description of his appearance came from. It seems the only direct encounter in the family happened to one of Mr Burrows' sons, Bert.

Bert Burrows, who had fought in the Middlesex Regiment during World War I, described what happened to the press:

> The ghost fairly put me through it. He bent over me and mesmerised me. I lay there as if paralysed. If you had

> said anything about ghosts two years ago I would have laughed. Now I don't.[4]

The encounter Burrows had sounded very much like an episode of sleep paralysis. As we have seen, sleep paralysis episodes appear to have been at the heart of a number of the ghost scares related in this book. Estimates vary as to how common these weird waking nightmares are, but somewhere between eight and forty per cent of the population will experience an episode of sleep paralysis in their lives.[5]

As the stories of the ghost spread through Uxbridge, more outlandish rumours began to emerge. One tale was that the ghost would light the family to bed, the ghost walking first with a light, followed by the family in single file behind him up the stairs. Another tall tale had it that rather than terrifying the horses in the adjoining stable, the ghost helpfully fed and groomed them.

Another episode reported in the press was the adventure of a local police sergeant who passed the Burrows' house in the small hours of the morning in early January. The officer noticed the figure of a man hanging over the garden gate. The sergeant politely wished the figure good night but received no answer. As he turned and looked at the figure again, he saw it had vanished. The sergeant was sure that the figure had been wearing a cap.[6]

As the new year progressed, the Uxbridge Ghost was becoming the talk of the town. Crowds of children began gathering outside the house on Cowley Road, sharing news, rumours, and tall tales about the ghost, and no doubt hoping to catch a glimpse of the apparition for themselves. Soon the size of the 'ghost flash mob' was such that the police were needed to maintain order. Among the crowds of children and the curious, there were also a gaggle of Spiritualists and psychic investigators, several of whom the Burrows invited into their home to try and bring an end to the phenomena. Although the family welcomed psychic investigators, they refused to allow journalists in. Therefore, many of the details in this episode were the result of a London journalist posing as a Spiritualist in order to gain entrance to the house and interview the family.[7]

We will now turn to some of these psychic investigations.

The New Year's Eve Seance

The first séance to try and contact the troublesome ghost was conducted by three friends of the Burrows family on Christmas Eve, 1921. The ghost's presence had often been felt in the stables, so the unnamed brave trio kept watch between nine in the evening and one in the morning on Christmas Day. Despite Christmas Eve being the time when every self-respecting ghost should be out haunting, the investigators watched in vain.

However, the same team of intrepid ghost busters tried again on New Year's Eve, with very different results. The three again spent the night in the stable sitting round a table, with one of the party sitting on a bin. As the night progressed, the lid of the bin the man was sitting on began to move, as if someone or something were inside it trying to get out, and at the same time the table began to 'play pranks'. Taking these events as a sign of the ghost's presence, the investigators decided now was the time to try to make contact with the spirit and find out who he was and why he was haunting the Burrows family.

The method used to communicate with the ghost was table turning. In this variation on the séance, the sitters would sit around a table with their hands resting on top. Then a question would be asked to the spirit and the letters of the alphabet would be slowly read out. The spirit would then supposedly make the table move at a certain letter, thus spelling out a message. However, in this particular séance on New Year's Eve 1921, the spirit was minded to spell out the answer to only one question. When the investigators, seated around their table, asked the spirit who he was, the twitching table spelt out the following name:

G-E-O-R-G-Z.[8]

The Hurdle Maker's Tale

Perhaps some psychic static had slightly garbled the communication between the living and the dead, for surely the ghost would be able to spell his own name. Perhaps, one report speculated, the ghost was just tired. In any case, it seemed obvious that the name 'George' was meant, and this was taken to mean that the spirit was that of one George Barnett who was thought to have lived in the house some fifty years ago.

Barnett was a hurdle maker, hurdles being a type of moveable sheep enclosure. Many locals in the area remember buying homemade fishing rods from him, though some accounts described Barnett as being short-tempered and of eccentric habits. Confusingly, it was also reported that George himself, while living in the house, had been haunted by a ghost who moved his hurdles mysteriously from one end of the yard to another. Who or what these 'invisible hands' belonged to is not revealed. These rumours gave rise to some speculation that George's ghost was attempting to lay the ghost that had been haunting him while he was alive.[9] In other words, George became a ghost in order to haunt the ghost that haunted him.

There were, though, some problems with the hypothesis identifying the Uxbridge Ghost with George Barnett. Firstly, it was revealed that it was not George Barnett who had once lived at the house on Cowley Road, but rather his brother James. Not only that, another spiritual communication (we are not given any details as to how this came about) claimed the ghost was called D-A-V-E.[10]

Furthermore, another candidate for the ghost's identity was about to emerge…

The Macaroni Parson's Tale

In a letter printed in the *Uxbridge and West Drayton Gazette* on 20 January, someone who signed him or herself K.C.H. suggested that the ghost might be the notorious man of letters, priest, dandy, and forger, William Dodd.[11] Dodd was born in Bourne, Lincolnshire in 1729 and after graduating from Cambridge University moved to London with the hope of starting a literary career. In 1751 Dodd married sixteen-year-old Mary Perkins, a daughter of a domestic servant. The lowly status of his wife led to a scandal and Dodd's father arranged for him to return to Cambridge and take up holy orders, which he eventually did while also pursuing his literary interests.

His greatest success was a book of Shakespeare's speeches published in 1752. This book, *The Beauties of Shakespeare*, had a brilliant innovation – an alphabetical list of all the topics covered in the speeches and the number of the page on which to find them. In other words, William Dodd had just invented the index. The book was still in print into the twentieth century.

Dodd became a popular priest, sometimes conducting worship for members of the royal family. Fortune certainly seemed to have been smiling on Dodd – in 1766, not only did his wife come into a substantial inheritance, but she also won £1000 on a lottery. This meant he had money to open Charlotte Chapel in Pimlico, London where the well-to-do attended his services. Dodd became known as a dandy, and his extravagant fashion sense led to him being nicknamed 'the Macaroni Pastor'. 'Macaroni' was a by word for trendy at the time, being associated with young aristocrats touring Europe and getting a taste for exotic Italian food. Dodd was involved in several high profile charitable causes such as support for fallen women, those in debt, and the Humane Society for the Resuscitation of Persons Apparently Drowned, which saved hundreds of people through various lifesaving techniques.[12]

William Dodd (portrait by John Russell, 1769)

Everything seemed to be going well for Dodd. He was a literary success, made a good living from his chapel and was comfortably off thanks to his wife's inheritance and lottery win. However, Dodd's extravagant way of life meant that despite his considerable income, his debts were mounting. In desperation, in 1774 he asked his wife to send an anonymous bribe to the Lord Chancellor's wife to try and get him appointed to Saint George's Chapel in Hanover Square, what would have been a lucrative position. The Lord Chancellor's wife showed the letter to her husband and it was traced back to Dodd. His reputation was in ruins and he fled to the continent to wait for the dust to settle.

When Dodd felt able to return to England he sold Charlotte Chapel for funds, but that still wasn't enough to keep him in the manner to which he was accustomed. One incident that prayed on his mind occurred in 1772 in Bromley. At a crossroads, he met an old gypsy woman who offered to tell his fortune if he crossed her palm with silver. Dodd dismissively sent her on her way, though as she departed, the gypsy seemed to curse him: 'Well, for all you're so proud, you'll be hanged at last.'[13] His fate was sealed when he forged a bond with his friend Lord Chesterfield.

The following day, Dodd happened to walk into a church service to hear the following words from Deuteronomy: 'And thy life shall hang in doubt before thee; and thou shalt fear day and night, and shall have none assurance for thy life.'[14] Dodd sat frozen in fear. Perhaps he knew he was doomed.

The forgery was detected and Dodd was arrested, confessing fully to his crime. He repaid most of the money and made arrangements to settle the amount that he'd already spent. Lord Chesterfield did not want to press charges against his friend, but Dodd's luck had now completely deserted him. The Lord Mayor insisted that Dodd be put on trial. The penalty for forgery was death. This was the height of the Bloody Code in which over three hundred and fifty capital crimes were on the statute books and people could be executed for stealing a handkerchief.[15]

As Dodd had confessed, the jury had to find him guilty, though they recommended leniency. The judge had no option but to impose the death penalty – Dodd was to hang for his crime. A petition on a parchment 37 yards long with 23,000 signatures asking for clemency was not enough to overturn the sentence, despite it being the greatest petition ever created. Nor was the intervention of famed writer and lexicographer Samuel Johnson enough to save Dodd from the hangman's noose.[16]

Dodd was held in Newgate Prison where he continued writing poetry. On 27 June 1777, he was taken to the gallows at Tyburn, where a large crowd had gathered for the spectacle. It seems there was some sympathy in the crowd for Dodd, and the spectators were unusually quiet and respectful. An ocean of black hats – thousands – were doffed in unison as Dodd passed. The sunshine fought with stormy squalls of rain as Dodd and a young lad called Harris prepared for their execution. Harris had stolen a few sovereigns and some silver, and the crowd was much upset at the sight of the condemned boy's distraught ageing father. A hood was placed over the boy's head, and Dodd had his hat and wig removed before a nightcap was placed on his head. The hangman did his job. The boy died quickly, though Dodd stretched his legs once or twice before falling still.

However, Dodd's friends had a cunning and audacious plan. They had arranged to take Dodd's body to a nearby surgeon where all the techniques for the resuscitation of drowned people that Dodd's charity had pioneered would be used to save the life of the parson. Unfortunately, the crowds were such that Dodd's friends had much difficulty getting past them to the surgeon's house. When they finally got Dodd's body to the surgery, air was pumped into his lungs, he was massaged with horseradish juice and turpentine and hot balsam was forced up his anus. They worked non-stop for two and a half hours, but the unfortunate Dodd remained dead.[17]

Dodd's remains were buried in the church at Cowley where his younger brother was rector.[18] So what links can be made between William Dodd and the spirit said to haunt the Burrow's house and stables? The letter writer (K.C.H.) offered a few suggestions to support his hypothesis. Firstly, Dodd has a connection with the local area. He is buried in a nearby church. Secondly, the New Year's Eve séance produced the name George (or 'Georgz'), and that was the name of the chapel that Dodd tried to bribe his way into, starting his precipitous fall from grace. Thirdly, the Uxbridge Ghost seems rather laconic when it comes to speaking through seances, and this may be because, after suffering so many criminal proceedings, Dodd's spirit does not want to be interrogated further. And finally, the overly harsh punishment Dodd received seems a good a reason as any to be a restless spirit, or as the letter writer puts it, to suffer from 'psychic insomnia'.[19]

The Medium's Tale

Whether the ghost was called George, Dave, or Dodd, the Burrows family wanted it gone. They had allowed some amateur seances in the stable on Christmas Eve and New Year's Eve but these had failed to stop the strange goings-on. Finally, it was the turn of an experienced medium to try to lay the ghost. Unfortunately, the name of the medium is not recorded, but as soon as she entered the family's house on Cowley Road, she claimed that she could see the spirit standing in the corner of the room. In fact, she said there was more than one spirit active in the house, which is probably not what the Burrows wanted to hear.

In any case, the medium had a talk with the troublesome ghost and found out the cause of his grievance, and received from the apparition the promise that if this grievance was dealt with, the haunting would cease. Frustratingly, the newspaper accounts don't give any more details about what this grievance was or how it was remedied, but the medium assured the family that the ghost that had been bothering them had now been escorted off the premises by some other spirits invoked for that purpose and back to the land of the dead. Mr Burrows and his wife and children could now, they hoped, look forward to a little peace.[20]

Epilogue

Or so they thought. It had been assumed that the medium had successfully evicted the ghost, but towards the end of January 1922 there were vague reports that it had returned. However, now the ghost was supposedly taking on a different form, though no details about what this may have been were released to the press or made public.

We are left with several unanswered questions, the most obvious being how did the ghost manifest itself when it returned? Was it George, Georgz, Dave, or William Dodd? Did the police sergeant really see a mysterious figure in a cap or was it his imagination playing tricks on him after a long nightshift? What terrified the horses that strange evening and prevented the stable door from being opened? What really happened in that New Year's Eve séance when the bin and table moved and the ghost supposedly spelled out his name? Was one of the party having a joke at the others' expense? Or – given that we are told the ghost was mainly felt or experienced in terms of cold blasts of air or household objects being moved from their proper place, could the real culprits behind the strange phenomena be one of the children playing pranks, with the draughty old house providing the ghostly chills? If this was the case, then when young Bert Burrows had an episode of apparent sleep paralysis in which he hallucinated a scary vision and felt paralysed, all these pieces could be put together creating a Christmas ghost story.

Chapter Eleven

Nurse Matilda ~ The Asylum Ghost

'One of the nurses tells me she tried to speak to the ghostly visitant, but she was too terrified to open her mouth. All who have seen the apparition agree in their description of its height, appearance and dress. They say it is clad as a nurse used to be towards the close of the last century.'
(Councillor Richard Taylor, Southend, 1923)

Bells rang, the gas lights dimmed, and then the towering spectral figure of Nurse Matilda, the spirit of a Victorian Poor Law Sister, would glide through the grounds of Rochford Hospital and Asylum in Essex. The nurses were terrified as an 'epidemic' of spooky sightings occurred between Christmas 1923 and January 1924, until one brave sister decided to crack the mystery of Nurse Matilda. But this ghost story has a rather prosaic twist...

Nurse Matilda ~ The Asylum Sister

The unlucky nurses working the Christmas and New Year night shifts of December 1922 and January 1923 at Rochford Hospital, Essex, were not happy. In fact, they were terrified – so terrified that some of the young probation nurses were threatening to quit. The object of their fear was an eerie phantom called Nurse Matilda, the towering spirit of a Poor Law Sister who had worked in the institution in Victorian times.

One of the most frightening aspects of this ghost was that its appearance was heralded by mysterious phenomena. First, the bells that connect all the rooms in the nurses' living quarters would start to ring. Then the lights in the corridors would dim. And from the gas lit gloom, a tall, strange female figure in Victorian nurse's uniform would appear, gliding across the hospital grounds, flitting down the shadowy corridors and then into the wards. This was Nurse Matilda, an eerie echo from the hospital's days as a Victorian workhouse and asylum. Matilda would stalk into the wards and inspect some of the patients' temperature charts before gliding away down the darkened corridors.[1]

According to Councillor Richard Taylor, member of the Rochford Guardians, in charge of governing the hospital, the ghost had appeared at various times for some years. Taylor told the press about some of the nurses' experiences with Matilda:

> One [nurse] states that on seeing it she tried to speak to it, but found that she was unable to articulate. Another nurse says she has seen 'Nurse Matilda', as the alleged ghost is called, on six occasions and twice recently.[2]

Taylor, who is described as a 'level-headed man', went on to describe the 'ghostly visitant':

All who have seen the apparition agree in their description of its height, appearance, and dress. They say it is clad as a nurse used to be towards the close of the last century.[3] On one occasion, a woman in the maternity ward encountered the ghost and asked it for a drink. The ghost refused and the patient made a complaint to the ward nurse.[4]

An unnamed hospital official described the nurses' state of mind as the stories of Nurse Matilda spread between Christmas and early January:

> Such was the state of nerves created among the nurses following the repetition of the story by the nurse who first saw the ghost that 'seeing ghosts' became an epidemic infection. We tried to laugh the nurses out of their visions, but they persisted, saying that they had seen the spectral night sister passing by the bedsides of the patients,

> looking at their temperature charts, and afterwards stealing silently out of the wards and disappearing in the gloom of the gas-lit corridors.[5]

There was a great deal of public interest in Nurse Matilda with one newspaper describing the whole town of Rochford as 'agog' at the mystery. Southend Spiritualists wanted to find out more about the haunting and offered to hold a séance in the hospital in order to question the ghost about why it was restlessly wandering the gloomy corridors and to help it find peace.[6] Others had more prosaic explanations for the phenomena. One possibility was that the 'ghost' was actually a patient from the newly added mental ward that was either being mistaken for a spirit or deliberately playing a joke. However, the attendants attested that none of their patients wandered around the hospital at night.

We are told that the doctors believed the nurses' stories, but thought that a practical joker was responsible, either a patient or more likely a member of staff. However, Councillor Richard Taylor, who did much to help the ghost story gain traction with his press interviews, found this explanation hard to believe. He thought it unlikely that a sick person, a nurse, or any other official would carry out such a prank.[7]

Rochford Hospital (rochforddistricthistory.org)

The Nurse's Tale

As January progressed, plans were made to catch Nurse Matilda. The Spiritualists' offer to hold a séance and question the ghost was not accepted. Instead, local residents clubbed together and put up a reward of £50 for the capture of anyone 'playing the ghost', more lights were lit in the hospital and a better watch kept.[8] These measures were successful, though it's not entirely clear what happened next. This is what transpired according to Edith Jones, the Superintendent Nurse. She was described as a nurse who 'was inclined to look for natural causes for "supernatural" events.'[9]

Nurse Jones hid in a dark room with a view of the hospital grounds and waited for the ghost to appear. Soon the ominous clang of the bell rang out through the building, and the corridor light flickered and dimmed. Miss Jones saw a spectral figure flit across the hospital grounds. She called a medical officer to be a witness. They watched and waited as the spirit approached the window of the room they were in, and then attempted to climb through it. The ghost was challenged and Nurse Jones' suspicions proved true. Nurse Matilda was a mental attendant called Edwin Jell and he had been caught red handed with a sheet over his head and his arms raised to make it appear that he was of abnormal height.[10]

On 23 January, Rochford Hospital Board of Guardians met to discuss the 'ghost'. Nurse Edith Jones was warmly thanked by the Board for her role in solving the mystery. The Board concluded that Edwin Jell should be dismissed immediately and they rejected his request for a month's salary, giving him only a 'qualified testimonial'. Jell had written a letter to be read out to the Board which showed he deemed the decision unfair:

> Considering the amount of foolery I have had to put up with, I think it is either an injustice or conspiracy to throw me out of employment.

However, the Chair of the Committee, Mr Dowsett, commented:

> The least we say about it the better. It is not the first time the man has been before the House Committee, and he had notice a few weeks ago that if any more nonsense occurred, he would be dismissed.

And dismissed he was, leaving the premises for good within the hour.[11] The ghost of Nurse Matilda no longer haunted the staff and patients of Rochford Hospital though it would return to haunt the courts...

The Ghost's Tale

Since losing his job at Rochford Hospital, Edwin Jell did not fare well and was unable to find work in the following years. Perhaps that was why in July 1927 he decided to sue his former employees for £25 pension contributions he had made while working at the hospital. This is what happened on the night he was caught, in his own words from the court hearing:

> Three years ago there were rumours that the institution was haunted. I had been reading the ghost story in a London paper, and as it was time for a night nurse to come on duty I threw a sheet over my shoulders and waited for her in the doorway. Presently, I heard footsteps, but instead of the nurse appearing it was the medical officer. He reported me to the committee and I was discharged.

Jell added:

> I was falsely blamed for the sins of someone else who had been acting the goat. I knew nothing about the Rochford ghost until I read about it in the newspapers. Once when

> the newspapers reported that the ghost had been seen, I was fifty miles away.

Jell denied Nurse Jones' claim that he had been seen in the grounds and wards with his arms over his head to make him appear abnormally tall. However, Miss Jones claimed she had also seen Jell dressed in a sheet in a corridor where patients suffering from 'mental derangement' would have seen him.

Jell's claim was that he had played a 'harmless joke' once and that the hospital Guardians were now robbing him of his pension contributions. The Guardians, for their part, claimed that he had paid less than £4 into his scheme. Judge Crawford heard the case and commented that it was of great public importance. The case was adjourned until September.[12]

Epilogue

So, was Edwin Jell a victim of a miscarriage of justice? Well, it seems that the ghostly apparitions stopped after he was sacked, but that doesn't mean that he was responsible for all the spooky sightings. It's certainly possible that other members of staff got up to similar antics and that poor old Edwin was made a scapegoat when things got out of hand and the probation nurses began threatening to quit. Oddly, some newspaper accounts at the time say that it was a female nurse who was caught playing the ghost and was dismissed all the while protesting her innocence, though this must be a reporting error.[13]

As well as the possibility that Jell was not the only hoaxer (and pretending to be a ghost and scaring people, as we have seen, was a common pastime in the nineteenth and early twentieth centuries), it's also plausible that some of the sightings were due to overactive imaginations among the young nurses. When the sightings started in the Christmas of 1922, it's quite possible that the nurses on the long wintery night shifts amused themselves with scary stories about Nurse Matilda stalking the wards. This may have led to the heightened nerves and the 'epidemic infection' of ghost sightings that followed.

In any case, Edwin Jell's case was dismissed in September 1926. The judge concluded that the case should have been brought within six months of the date of the dismissal. Furthermore, the court decided that the Guardians had acted properly in their summary dismissal of Jell.

The court found that pretending to be a ghost was indeed 'grave misconduct'.[14]

Chapter Twelve

The Clanking Ghost of East Barnet

'I was standing by my hut at twelve o'clock, and I heard a strange noise at my back. I looked round and there was what appeared to be a man dressed in a heavy cavalry coat. What struck me as exceeding strange was that I could see a skeleton in the coat....'

(Charles Anthony Gibson, 1926)

The Clanking Ghost of East Barnet was said to be the restless spirit of Sir Geoffrey de Mandeville a wicked outlaw baron from the twelfth century. His ghost was rumoured to appear in the village every Christmas, causing a sensation as crowds of hundreds and then thousands would gather to try and catch sight of him, or perhaps to hear the ghostly clanging of his spurs and armour. The Clanking Ghost of East Barnet is a true tale of spooky sightings and mysterious noises that takes a turn for the romantic when the ghost gets a girlfriend, and a turn for the surreal when the local council becomes involved...

The Clanking Ghost of East Barnet

It was a cold December night in 1926. In the village of East Barnet, now a suburb of London, but then still quite rural, a dilapidated old house called 'the Shanty' stood on the site of one of the oldest workhouses in England. According to local legend, the workhouse's crumbling cellars still hid the bones of young orphans lost in the labyrinthine underground passages, or perhaps locked there and forgotten about for some minor misdemeanour. On this particular evening, two elderly ladies and their pet dog were huddling around the old-fashioned fireplace in the old-fashioned sitting room of this gloomy house as midnight approached. The dog started and pricked up his ears. Heavy footsteps were thudding down the hallway accompanied by a weird clanking sound reminiscent of jangling spurs or perhaps the sound of ancient armour. The women lived alone and no one could possibly be in their house but themselves. They opened the door to the hallway, but there was no one to be seen. They searched the house but found nothing.

As midnight approached the following night, no doubt the two elderly ladies and their pet felt some trepidation. And with good reason, for soon the familiar thump of footsteps accompanied by the clang of metal was heard in the hallway. This time, though, the footsteps came to the sitting room door and then halted. There followed a loud banging on the door.

The petrified dog whimpered and cowered under the table. The ladies cautiously approached the door and, turning the handle, saw... nothing.

Every night the ominous thuds and dolorous clangs were heard passing along the hallway followed by thumping on the door.

This was the Clanking Ghost of East Barnet.

The story was widely reported in the newspapers in December 1926, though no information is given about who the (suspiciously anonymous) haunted old women were or what the source was for the story of the clanking footsteps and ghostly knocking. We are, though, told who the clanking ghost was – Geoffrey de Mandeville, a powerful twelfth-century nobleman turned rebel and outlaw.[1]

Geoffrey de Mandeville was an important figure in the time of the English Civil War known as 'the anarchy' when King Stephen's rule was challenged by the Empress Matilda. De Mandeville's grandfather was a companion of William the Conqueror, and his father was the constable of the Tower of London which Geoffrey inherited from him. Geoffrey de Mandeville flirted with both sides of the civil war and through political intrigue became one of the richest and most powerful nobles in the land. It was even said that his power rivalled that of the king. In 1143 his duplicitous support for King Stephen's rival for the throne the Empress Matilda led to him being publicly accused of treason. He was arrested and forced to give up the Tower of London and his castles or face execution.

With the source of much of his power gone, Geoffrey was freed, though now he was in furious open revolt against the king. He stormed off to the English fens – a traditional hideout for rebels – where he seized Ramsey Abbey for his headquarters and built a new power base as an outlaw, conducting violent raids on Cambridge and surrounding towns. The hostile fens made it hard for King Stephen to find the outlaw, but they finally met in battle in 1144 where Geoffrey received an arrow to the head and died soon after.

Because he had desecrated and plundered church property, Geoffrey had been excommunicated and could not be interred in hallowed ground. For twenty years his casket lay unburied in the Old Temple in Holborn before his son finally managed to gain absolution for his father's sins and his remains were buried at the New Temple.[2] However, some legends say that Geoffrey de Mandeville drowned in nearby Camlet Moat, a small-moated island North of London. Hidden in the deepest part of the moat is said to be Geoffrey's treasure – a chest full of gold and jewels chained to the bottom of the moat. It seems there were stories of Geoffrey's ghost stalking the environs of the moat before he came to bother the good people of Barnet.[3] And there was much more to come from this noisy ghost.

Camlet Moat (Geograph.org.uk)

The Ghost and the Council

Shortly before Christmas 1926 council nightwatchman Charles Anthony Gibson warmed his hands in front of his brazier as he guarded equipment being used on some road repairs. The nightwatchman's little hut was on a windy lane not far from the dilapidated house where the unnamed elderly ladies had heard the mysterious clanking footsteps. On one side of the lonely lane was a crumbling ruin wreathed in ivy, and on the other a grotesque gnarled old oak tree. Gibson himself takes up the story:

> I was standing by my hut at twelve o'clock, and I heard a strange noise at my back. I looked round and there was what appeared to be a man dressed in a heavy cavalry coat. What struck me as exceeding strange was that I could see a skeleton in the coat…[4]

Gibson's blood ran cold. Could the hideous skeletal figure in the military coat be the clanking ghost of East Barnet – Geoffrey de Mandeville?

In any case, one of Gibson's workmates told the *Daily News* that his mate was convinced he had seen something supernatural. 'He is a teetotaller... and was so sure about it that he made me quite nervous', he said.[5] Gibson was apparently too shaken to continue his watch and his place was taken by another.

However, the Clanking Ghost had not escaped the notice of the East Barnet urban district council. At a council meeting, in reference to the watchman's experience, one member pointed out that council workers carrying out employment that was 'exceptionally disagreeable' were entitled to an extra shilling's pay in compensation. The council member then asked whether this extra compensation would be made available to the council nightwatchman on duty near a haunted house. The chairman replied that it was the surveyor who should make the decision as to what would count as 'exceptionally disagreeable' and who should investigate the matter and report back to the council.[6]

Reports in the press of the ghastly skeletal spook brought the odd curiosity seeker to the nightwatchman's hut the following night, hoping to catch a glimpse of the ghost. A number of journalists also turned up and reported on the vigil. One described his experience for the *Daily News*, saying the narrow winding lane was 'ideal for ghosts' with its ruins, gnarled oaks and a 'waste of dreary land'. Between eleven and midnight the journalist and nightwatchman saw nothing unusual. At midnight a youth turned up looking for the ghost, followed soon after by a man with a big stick who was also determined to see Sir Geoffrey.

As they waited a dark figure appeared by a disused well and looked to be searching inside it. The figure approached the party and it turned out to be another youth who with his friend had been looking to see if there were any ghosts in the well. There were not. At two in the morning, the journalist gave up and left to phone his story into the office, leaving the youth and the man with the big stick to continue their watch.[7]

The following day, there was some concern over the council's decision to consider paying the nightwatchmen extra to compensate for the possibility of seeing a ghost. The *Western Daily Press*, for example, considered the dangers of granting a financial bonus as a reward for 'seeing things' and the implications that may have for the council budget and local taxes.[8]

The interest in the Clanking Ghost was such that East Barnet Urban District Council felt obliged to issue a statement to the press to the effect that the surveyor had been instructed to investigate the watchmen's wages. The surveyor had not been instructed to investigate the existence of the ghost. The nightwatchman himself was quoted as saying, 'It's all untrue. I never saw a ghost.'[9] It's not clear why he retracted his story or even if it was the same nightwatchman – Gibson – that had described the bony phantom, as his name is rarely given in the reports. It's certainly possible that an enthusiastic journalist invented or embellished the story. It's also possible that Gibson made up the story as a lark to tell his mates, but that the prank had now got out of hand, dragging in the council, its surveyor, the media, and the curious public. However, these clarifications and denials did not lay the ghost, nor did they assuage public and media interest in the haunting.

The story was just too good to let go. It had a characterful ghost of a powerful feudal villain, a spooky atmospheric setting and even a touch of local council comic relief. One newspaper, the *Liverpool Echo*, celebrated the appearance of Geoffrey – a proper, old-fashioned type of Christmas ghost:

> It is hard work clanking and swanking about in armour, and there are some shirkers in the ghost world who are content with a white sheet.

The article continues to suggest that a benefit be held to support the ghost and to raise some money so that he can oil his rusty centuries old armour.[10]

On the next night, 22 December, many more people gathered in the narrow street hoping to see Geoffrey de Mandeville. Nothing was seen, but there was some excitement when three unnamed witnesses arrived in a car telling the assembled ghost hunters that they had been about a mile away at Camlet Moat, the place where legend says Geoffrey drowned (or had drowned himself) and they had seen the ghost crossing the moat bridge. They described the ghost as 'a very tall man with long hair, who was wearing a long mantle. Light tinkling sounds accompanied his walking movement.'[11]

But in that strange interregnum between Christmas and New Year, even more ghostly secrets would be unearthed.

The Magistrate's Tale

Mr Walter Stutters was a Justice of the Peace and an old resident of East Barnet. He came forward to confirm that he too had visited the Shanty where the spectral footsteps had been heard and that he also had heard uncanny noises – rumblings, tappings, muffled voices, and a strange jingling which seemed to run around the room. He had also seen things:

> Further, on one occasion I saw before me quite plainly a spirit, and looking at it closely I saw through it, and was able to distinguish objects on the other side. It gradually passed away, leaving no trace.

Stutters went on to describe the effect that the haunted house had on visitors:

> I have seen strong men walk away from the house with wide-staring eyes and trembling limbs as though their

> knees would refuse to support their bodies, because of this experience. Women have been seen to hurry away wrapping their cloaks and shawls about them, seemingly anxious to get away from the scenes they have witnessed…

If anyone didn't believe what he said, Stutters invited them to visit the house and test the matter for themselves. The owners, Stutters claimed, welcome interested visitors – though children were not allowed to enter for fear of the dire consequences the experience would have on their tender minds.[12]

But at this point, the story takes a rather romantic turn.

Night of the Loving Dead ~ Geoffrey and the Grey Lady

On New Year's Eve, many British papers reported some heart-warming seasonal news – a 'spectral romance'. The *Daily Mirror* wrote that Geoffrey de Mandeville, the 'wicked' Earl of Essex, had been joined by another ghost. She was called the Grey Lady and haunted the Grange, an oak-panelled Georgian House and its surrounds on Church Hill Road. The Lady was described as aristocratic and very beautiful, with a charming dimpled smile. She was wrapped in a flowing grey cloak from which she got her name. It was rumoured among the locals, according to the press, that the Grey Lady's mission was to 'placate Geoffrey's restless spirit', and to offer herself in marriage.[13]

The Grey Lady had, it seems, originally haunted an 'old clock house' near the Grange, but when that was demolished she had become restless and began to haunt the Grange and the surrounding village. It's not always clear which houses the press refer to and there seems to be some confusion between the Grange and the Shanty and which ghosts belonged where.[14] In any case, the Grey Lady's reputed beauty began to attract admirers, as well as the usual gaggle of journalists, investigators and curiosity seekers. One newspaper commented on how the way we view ghosts had changed:

> In the old days, when a house had the reputation of being haunted, everybody gave it a wide berth. In these more inquisitive times, people do not flee in terror; they want to come in and see the ghost.[15]

And come they did. East Barnet's reputation as a haunting hot spot was drawing in the crowds. They came not just to see Geoffrey now, but were also drawn by the Grey Lady's 'considerable personal attractions, including dimples in her ghostly cheeks.'[16] On Thursday 30 December a reporter from the *Mirror* wrote that two policemen were attempting to control a crowd of 'ardent psychic investigators'. On the 4 January 1927, the *Edinburgh Evening News* reported that hundreds were visiting the village in search of ghosts and that the roads were blocked. Extra police had to be drafted in to control the crowds and regulate the traffic.[17]

Journalists, no doubt happy to keep the story running, joined in the ghost hunts and investigations. One interviewed the present occupier of the Grange, Mr R. Marshall who was understandably annoyed at being asked about ghosts all day. He confirmed that his house had 'deep, dark cellars', which is only what one would expect from a haunted house, but denied that he had ever seen a ghost. 'I am fed up with the ghost,' he said. 'I am referring everyone to Sir Oliver Lodge and the College of Psychic Science.'[18] Oliver Lodge was a distinguished physicist who, like his contemporaries journalist, W.T. Stead and author, Arthur Conan Doyle, became obsessed with mediums and Spiritualism.[19]

A few days later, Mr Marshall's patience was further tried. When a journalist knocked on the door, a window was thrown open and a voice cried: '`Op it. Go to `ell. Send for Conan Doyle. Don't come round `ere.'[20] The intrepid reporter from the *Mirror* spent several nocturnal hours hiding in the shrubbery near what he thought was a secret entrance to the mysterious passages that ran under the house – the passages with the ghostly shades of hungry orphans. Nothing exciting happened until the witching hour:

> At midnight a supernatural roar disturbed the silence of the night. My hair stood on end and I shivered. There was a rattle of hoofs… It was not a ghost. It was a donkey![21]

But as the first few days of January 1927 wore on, the magic wore off and Geoffrey and the Grey Lady, along with the ghost hunters melted into the winter…

Return of the Ghost

On Christmas Eve 1928 a large crowd of ghost hunters and thrill seekers descended on East Barnet. This was becoming an annual event. The ghost of Geoffrey de Mandeville was now associated with this season of the year, and it must have been a carnivalesque atmosphere on this festive ghost hunt. Two policemen were needed to regulate the extra traffic the ghost was attracting, and the crowd – made up of both believers and sceptics – was described as particularly lively. There were cameramen, people carrying flashlights and 'noisy youths' carrying pitchforks and rakes. One might also suspect that Geoffrey de Mandeville was not the only spirit at work that night.

Although the Christmas Eve ghost hunting flash mob was rather impromptu, the New Barnet Research Society was more organised. This was a society set up to make contact with Geoffrey's ghost. As explained by an unnamed member of the Society:

> The purpose of the Research Society is to get into communications with the ghost quietly and try, if possible, to find out why Sir Geoffrey's spirit remained earthbound… Once we find out the cause we hope to make it easier for the spirit to go to the other side.

The Research Society had also received offers of help from a party of army officers. One officer wrote:

> Any personal discomfort to which I may be put in hunting the ghost matters nothing. I do not fear any ghost, and if I get any shock or damage, I alone am responsible.

The secretary of the Society had to decline the gallant offers by the military men. One reason was that the Society didn't want to appear confrontational to Sir Geoffrey should they meet him, and the appearance of military men may have been perceived as aggressive by the ghost.

The Society posted volunteers at various haunted locations in the village on several nights over the Christmas period. One of these volunteers was an anonymous London Spiritualist who declined to give his name and address to the press. This is his story:

> A few minutes before twelve o'clock, near the old parish church at East Barnet, I saw in the distance a vague figure dressed in a heavy cloak, moving towards me in the direction of the Farm Home. I stood still and waited for this to approach, but suddenly it seemed to pass through a wall and disappear in the fields in the direction of Trent Barnet. As I waited and listened I distinctly heard sounds like the clanking of spurs, but saw nothing more of the strange figure.

Soon after midnight the suspiciously anonymous Spiritualist drove back to London, his spooky experience making his belief in spirits even stronger.[22]

In the days before New Year's Eve, members of Barnet's Research Society were becoming despondent. Firstly, many of their members had fallen ill with heavy colds, blamed on their nocturnal ghost hunts in wintery weather conditions. Secondly, there was the ghost's failure to appear – at least to any of the Research Society's members. The only supposed witness to a ghost this season was the unnamed London Spiritualist. The local ghost hunters, according to press reports, were feeling somewhat slighted.[23] Perhaps they were resentful of the way outsiders – mediums, Spiritualists, army officers and the curious public – were muscling in on their ghost.

But in early January 1929, another organisation was again taking an interest in the Clanking Ghost of East Barnet – the Council.

Return of the Council

Five residents of East Barnet were not happy with the rates the council had imposed on their properties. On 15 January 1929, they appealed for a reduction, and the council again raised the ghost. Mr Rourke of the council committee asked Mr Deamer of the rating authority the all-important question: 'Is there a ghost there?'

Mr Deamer replied: 'We have not rated the ghost's residence'.

The claimants succeeded in obtaining a £3 rebate, though it's not clear from the reports if the residents were claiming the rebate because of the ghost, nor if the reason for the granting of the rebate was the ghost.[24]

Nevertheless, after this brief cameo at another council meeting, the ghost of Geoffrey de Mandeville hung up his spurs and armour for another season.

Dogs, Drums and Spirit Manifestations

As Christmas 1929 approached, the dogs of East Barnet and district began to grow restless when darkness fell. As we saw when Sir Geoffrey visited the old ladies in the Shanty a few years ago, dogs seemed to dislike or fear this clanking spirit. And clanking was not the only noise associated with Geoffrey.

An unnamed woman told the press that on two consecutive nights she had heard the sound of muffled drums coming from the 'ghost centre' (meaning by the moat in which Geoffrey was traditionally thought to have drowned).

The Barnet Research Society was on the case. They had their investigators holding vigil at various ghostly hotspots in East Barnet and South Mimms, with telephone communication arranged between them. The Society declared that 'spirit manifestations' had occurred in both these locations.

However, the Society was not happy. It seems members were still resentful that the only noteworthy ghost appearance last season was that witnessed by an anonymous London Spiritualist. This season, the Society decided to keep their investigation in-house and announced they were going to ignore London psychical researchers. The Society also felt that they had been crowded out by the hordes of Londoners descending on the village in their cars with cameras and lamps.[25] No doubt many in these crowds were full of festive cheer and out for a lark, and perhaps not taking the investigation as seriously as the Barnet Research Society would have liked.

Undeterred by big city psychic investigators, Spiritualists, and enthusiastic crowds of thrill-seekers, the Barnet Research Society would continue its attempts to make contact with the ghostly inhabitants of the region for years to come. The appearance of Geoffrey de Mandeville, the Clanking Ghost of East Barnet (along with a cast of various supporting spirits) and the subsequent nocturnal ghost hunts had become an established annual tradition.

Hysterical Folk Barred from Christmas Ghost Hunt

In late December 1932 the Barnet Research Society issued a report announcing that in recent days the spirit of Geoffrey de Mandeville had been 'plainly seen' at Oak Hill. The appearance of the ghost was heralded by 'subdued martial music, the clank of steel, and the sound of marching men'. The ghost of old Geoffrey seemed to be putting a band together. Within a few years, he had gone from jangling his spurs and clanging his armour, to muffled drums, martial music, and marching men.

However, although the Christmas hunt for Geoffrey's ghost was an annual event, the Research Society was adamant that the ghost's appearance was not. As the report said:

> It can now be definitely stated from many years' experience that the Mandeville spirit manifestation occurs every six years. The last visitation was Christmas Eve, 1926. Many scoffers came to East Barnet to jeer and deride, and returned to their homes sadder but wiser men.[26]

It's not clear what was meant by the last comments. Perhaps it was suggesting that the sceptical thrill-seekers had actually seen a ghost and that had made them 'sadder but wiser', or that they had come during the ghost's six-year sabbatical and so been disappointed. In any case, their claim that the ghost only appeared every six years allowed the Research Society to nimbly dismiss the claims made by London Spiritualists and psychic investigators, as the last true sighting was in 1926.

With six years now elapsed since the 1926 visits of the ghost, the Barnet Research Society announced plans for its investigations. The Society planned to meet at 10.45pm at the junction with Brook Hill Road, Cat Hill 'and proceed by stealth to the haunts of the spirit at Oak Hill.' The seriousness with which the Society undertook their investigation is underlined by their injunction to members not to invite 'hysterical persons' along on their ghost hunt.

We don't really know the result of the Society's investigations that season, though some newspapers did publish a report by an anonymous correspondent claiming to have witnessed one of the hunts. We are not told on which particular night the correspondent joined the hunt, though it was both cold and cloudy:

> There was a woodland copse in the background. As we stood, staring, there was a sudden break in the clouds and there could be seen clearly a figure in armour – Sir Geoffrey de Mandeville.

The tongue-in-cheek correspondent also claimed to have found a dozen people in the village who had seen a similar sight three times in the last twenty years.[27]

However, when Christmas 1933 rolled around, the six year rule was conveniently forgotten and thousands were heading to East Barnet and South Mimms to join the Research Society in its ongoing attempts to contact Sir Geoffrey. Now, though, the Research Society had another distraction to contend with: film crews whose bright lights were threatening to 'spoil the show'.[28] The fear was that all the crowds, equipment, cameras and lights might scare away the ghost.

A similar fear was expressed the following Christmas Eve when camera crew and members of the public were told to keep well hidden behind bushes so as not to scare away the spirit. By now Sir Geoffrey's ghost had an established promenade down an old track, and this was where, ironically, the thrill-seekers, psychic investigators, Christmas revellers, journalists and camera crews haunted the ghost.[29] When Sir Geoffrey's clanking Christmas appearances were reported in 1926, the old ladies and their dog cowered in their shanty, and the nightwatchman who saw his skeletal phantom was so scared the council considered paying a ghost bonus. Within a few years, it was the ghost himself who was being haunted.

Epilogue

Another ghost hunt and vigil was attempted on Christmas Eve in 1945. A thousand cars from all over London crowded into East Barnet, and over 400 people waited at Pym's Brook in the cold December darkness to catch a glimpse of the ghost. The December mist was all they saw.[30]

Sir Geoffrey was an elusive and fickle ghost, though his story does leave open the possibility of love and redemption. Perhaps the dimpled charms of the Grey Lady won him over, he repented his past misdeeds and has hung up his clanking spurs.

Stocking Fillers

Shorn of the Dead ~ Shaving Corpses at Christmas

'... horror of horrors – the mouth slightly opened, and an unearthly "oh-h-h" from the dead man made all start back in fright...'

(*Gateshead Observer*, 1879)

In times past it was common for a corpse to be shaved before burial. Few self-respecting Christian men would want to meet their maker with several days' growth of stubble; they would want to look their very best. The following two supposedly true anecdotes were published on Christmas Eve 1879 and 1885, and both concern men who find themselves with the unenviable task of shaving a corpse at Christmas...

The Preacher's Tale

This 'singular Christmas Eve experience' took place in the late 1830s in a nameless Lincolnshire village.[1]

It was the night before Christmas and snow covered the roads and roofs of the village. An itinerant methodist preacher arriving in the settlement on a visit was struck by something odd – the streets were eerily deserted. On Christmas Eve there would normally be a bustling festive atmosphere, but not a soul was to be seen. Perplexed, the preacher proceeded to the house he was visiting and was told by his host the reason for the empty streets – Old Jones was dead.

Old Jones was the village patriarch, a much-respected stalwart of the local community. He was known by all, and his loss was deeply felt. However, there was another worry on the minds of the villagers – on his deathbed Old Jones had expressed the wish that he be shaved before burial. The old man had shaved every Saturday night or Sunday morning to look his best for church, for in those days it was quite common to only shave once or twice a week and daily shaving was rare. In any case, Old Jones wanted to look his best when he met his maker, and everyone wanted to honour his last request. The problem was, there was no barber in the village and all the other men were either too superstitious or squeamish to touch the corpse. The village women were made of sterner stuff and were ready to take on the duty, but none of them had handled a razor before.

The preacher saw how much this meant to the villagers and, after some hesitation, offered to shave Old Jones himself. The host took the preacher to the house of Old Jones's family, and they were much relieved to hear that someone would carry out this final office for Jones so that he would not be buried unshaven like a heathen. The family handed the preacher Old Jones's shaving box and razors, the ones he'd used every week without fail during his long life, and the preacher along with a couple of lady friends of the family ascended the stairs to the room where the corpse of Old Jones waited.

As they opened the door to the bedroom, the candle cast a pale and flickering light over the chill gloom. There on the bed were the mortal remains of Old Jones looking grim and haggard in death after his many years of hard work followed by his long illness. But his week's growth of stubble made him look 'beggarly, blackguardly'.

The preacher steadied his nerves and approached the bed. The closer he got, the more ghastly the face of Old Jones appeared in the weak glimmer of the candle flame. With the ladies by his side, the preacher lathered up the shaving brush, took a breath, and then applied it to the grizzled face in a few swift strokes. Now with the lower half of his face smeared in shaving foam, the old man looked even worse – like a wicked Santa Claus.

The preacher was unsure if he was shivering due to the chill of the room or from the dread of what he had to do next. The ladies passed him the razor, and after a moment's hesitation, he prepared to make the first stroke and grasped the corpse's lips. According to the report: 'Horror of horrors – the mouth slightly opened and an unearthly "oh-h-h" from the dead man made all start back in fright.'

The candle fell to the floor and sputtered out and the ladies and the preacher scrambled around in the darkness trying to find the door. They found it and flung it open stumbling and falling over one another down the narrow corridor and staircase. The women screamed in terror, thinking the dead man was behind them clawing at their dresses. They didn't stop until they were outside pale and quivering in the snowy street.

The screaming brought the neighbours out of their houses. After hearing what had happened, a few brave villagers elected to go inside to investigate and a new candle was brought. They crept up the narrow staircase and peered into the room. There was Old Jones lying in the same position, still looking like a ghoulish Father Christmas. There was no sign of movement.

It was decided that when the preacher had taken hold of the dead man's lips, it caused gasses to escape from the body producing the ghostly groan that had sent everyone flying in terror.

Old Jones was sent on his final journey clean shaven just as he had wished.

The Barber's Tale

The following report appeared in the *Yorkshire Gazette* on Christmas Eve 1885, though the events supposedly happened in the middle of the nineteenth century.[2]

Old Curler ran an old-fashioned barber's shop at the Oxford Street end of Tottenham Court Road in London. He was rather a crusty old Tory, according to Bob his apprentice, who said that Old Curler affected the manners of a toff and was such a snob that he would turn away custom from his shop if he thought the client was not of sufficient social standing.

One of the regular customers was Captain Blazer, who came for his shave at nine o'clock every morning without fail. It was always Bob's duty to attend to the Captain, a job he did not relish in the least. Captain Blazer had a blazing temper, and the slightest nick would set him roaring furious oaths in Bob's face.

However, one morning Captain Blazer didn't appear. A few days later, Old Curler was told that the Captain had passed away. And what's more, in his will he stipulated that before burial he should be shaved at the usual hour. This was not a duty that Old Curler was keen to do, so it fell to the poor apprentice. It was only right, Old Curler explained, that Bob should carry out the duty as he had done every day when the Captain was alive. Bob was horrified at the prospect, but he needed his position and reluctantly agreed.

The next day a trepidatious Bob called at the Captain's house in Bedford Square shortly before nine. The housekeeper invited him in and briskly ushered him into the room with the Captain and shut the door on him. The Captain lay looking as furious in death as he had in life. Bob poured some hot water into the shaving bowl, covered the brush in foam all the while dreading his first touch of the dead man. Finally, after shrinking back a couple of times, he managed to splash a blob of the foam on the Captain's chin. He then proceeded to cover the Captain's stubble with the lather, then picked up his razor with trembling hand.

As he started to scrape the stubble from the corpse's cheek, Bob couldn't help thinking back on all the times the Captain had berated him with foul-mouthed abuse when he had given him a cut. These thoughts made his hands shake even more until inevitably he caused a gash across the Captain's face. Through force of habit, the young apprentice said, 'I beg your pardon, sir; it shan't occur again.'

As he turned to get a towel, he heard an all too familiar voice boom 'Confound you, sir, what the dickens d'ye mean by cutting me like this? I'll complain to your master, sir, and have you discharged as incompetent – I will, damme, sir.'

The Captain was sitting bolt upright in bed, dabbing at his bleeding cheek with a handkerchief and glaring at the astounded apprentice. The Captain had, so it seemed, been in a coma or some kind of cataleptic trance (the report is vague on this) and the clumsy apprentice's razor had brought him round and saved the Captain from the horrible fate of being buried alive.

The Captain became a regular customer again at Old Curler's for many years after that. As for Bob, the Captain was so grateful that he paid for him to go to New Zealand and set up his own barber's shop in Auckland. Though in all his career, Bob swore he would never again 'shave a dead 'un.'

Epilogue

How much truth there is in these two newspaper stories is hard to say. They both sound like they could be urban legends and were probably inserted into Christmas Eve editions of the newspapers for a bit of dark festive fun and ghoulish black humour.

End Notes

Introduction

1 Owen Davies, *The Haunted* (London: Palgrave Macmillan, 2007) p.131

2 Paul Weatherhead, *Weird Calderdale* (Hebden Bridge: Tom Bell Publishing, 2023) pp.11–45

Chapter 1: The Hammersmith Ghost

1 *Hampshire Chronicle,* 11 August 1800, p.3; *Newcastle Courant,* 16 August 1800, p.2

2 Jacob Middleton, *Spirits of an Industrial Age* (2018) p.7

3 Jeremy Harte, 'Maimed Rites: Suicide Burials in the English Landscape', *Time and Mind,* 4:2 (2011) pp.263–282, doi: 10.2752/175169711X13046099195438

4 Martin Puhvel, 'The Mystery of the Cross Roads', *Folklore,* 87:2 (1976) pp.167–177, doi: 10.1080/0015587X.1976.9716030

5 Harte (2011)

6 Harte (2011)

7 Edward Walford, 'Hammersmith', in *Old and New London: Volume 6* (London, 1878), pp. 529–548; *British History Online* http://www.british-history.ac.uk/old-new-london/vol6/pp529-548 [accessed: 8 July 2023].

8 R.S. Kirby, *Kirby's Wonderful and Scientific Museum Volume 2* (London, 1804), p.76

9 *Ibid*

10 *Ibid*

11 'The Ghost of Hammersmith', *Morning Post,* 6 January 1804, p.3

12 'Murder – Hammersmith Ghost', *Saint James's Chronicle,* 14 January 1804, p.3

13 See for example the painting *Two Boys with a Bladder* by Joseph Wright of Derby available at: https://www.getty.edu/art/collection/object/109Q0X about 1769–1770

14 'The Ghost of Hammersmith', *Morning Post,* 6 January 1804, p.3

15 'The Real Hammersmith Ghost', *Oracle and Daily Advertiser,* 9 January 1804, p.3

16 'Melancholy Catastrophe', *Saint James's Chronicle,* 5 January 1804, p.4

17 'Melancholy Accident', *Sun (London),* 5 January 1804, p.3

18 'The Real Hammersmith Ghost', *Oracle and Daily Advertiser,* 9 January 1804, p.3

19 Kirby (1804) pp.77–78

20 *Ibid* p.79

21 *Ibid* p.66

22 'The Ghost of Hammersmith', *Morning Post,* 6 January 1804, p.3

23 'Coroner's Inquest', *London Courier and Evening Gazette,* 6 January 1804, p.3

24 *Ibid*

25 'Murder – Hammersmith Ghost', *Saint James's Chronicle,* 14 January 1804, p.3; 'Murder', *True Briton,* 14 January 1804, pp.3–4

26 'Coroner's Inquest', *London Courier and Evening Gazette,* 6 January 1804, p.3

27 'Melancholy Catastrophe', *Saint James's Chronicle,* 5 January 1804, p.4

28 'The Real Hammersmith Ghost', *Oracle and Daily Advertiser,* 9 January 1804, p.3

29 *Ibid*

30 Kirby (1804) p.79

31 'The Real Hammersmith Ghost', *Oracle and Daily Advertiser.* 9 January 1804, p.3

32 *Ibid*

33 Kirby (1804) p.79

34 'Murder – Hammersmith Ghost', *Saint James's Chronicle,* 14 January 1804, p.3

35 *Ibid*

36 *Morning Chronicle,* 25 January 1804, p.3

37 *London Chronicle,* 19 July 1804, p.2

38 'Real Hammersmith Ghost Found', *Oracle and Daily Advertiser,* 26 January 1804, p.2

39 Kirby (1804) p.79

40 *Oracle and Daily Advertiser,* 11 January 1804, p.3

41 'The Hammersmith Ghost, a Spiritual Drunkard', *Globe,* 17 January 1837, p.3

Chapter 2: The Hammersmith Monster

1 'A New Hammersmith Ghost', *Morning Herald,* 3 December 1824, p.2; 'The New Hammersmith Ghost', *Morning Advertiser*, 7 December 1824, p.3

2 'The New Hammersmith Ghost', *Morning Advertiser,* 7 December 1824, p.3

3 'The New Hammersmith Ghost', *Morning Advertiser,* 23 December 1824, p.3; 'The New Hammersmith Ghost', *Morning Herald*, 24 December 1824, p.4

4 Jan Bondeson, *The London Monster: A Sanguinary Tale* (Da Capo Press, 2002))

5 'The New Hammersmith Ghost', *Morning Advertiser,* 23 December 1824, p.3

6 'The New Hammersmith Ghost', *Morning Herald,* 24 December 1824, p.4

7 'The New Hammersmith Ghost', *Morning Herald,* 28 January 1825, p.4

8 *Ibid*

9 W. Brown, *Pierce Egin's Life in London and Sporting Guide,* 6 February 1825, p.5

10 'A Ghost Taken!', *Morning Advertiser,* 18 February 1825, p.3; 'Capture of the Hammersmith Ghost', *The News,* 20 February 1825, p.5

11 'A Ghost Taken!', *Morning Advertiser,* 18 February 1825, p.3

12 'A Ghost Taken!', *Morning Advertiser,* 18 February 1825, p.3; 'Capture of the Hammersmith Ghost', *The News,* 20 February 1825, p.5

13 'A Ghost Taken!', *Morning Advertiser,* 18 February 1825, p.3

14 'Resuscitation of the Hammersmith Ghost', *Morning Post,* 12 December 1833, p.2

15 Paul Weatherhead, *Weird Calderdale* (Hebden Bridge: Tom Bell Publishing, 2023)

16 'The New Hammersmith Ghost', *Morning Herald,* 28 January 1825, p.4

17 'Resuscitation of the Hammersmith Ghost', *Morning Post,* 12 December 1833, p.2

18 'Autobiography of the Hammersmith Ghost', *Fraser's Magazine for Town and Country,* Vol XVIII, 1838, pp.338–347

19 Jacob Middleton *Spirits of an Industrial Age* (2018), p.68

Chapter 3: The Peterborough Poltergeist

1 'Mysterious Manifestations in a Peterborough Cottage', *Buckingham Advertiser and Free Press,* 16 January 1892, p.3

2 *Ibid*

3 *Ibid*

4 'Ghosts at Peterborough', *Gloucester Citizen,* 9 January 1892, p.3

5 'The Alleged Haunted House', *Peterborough Express,* 13 January 1892, p.3

6 'Mysterious Manifestations in a Peterborough Cottage', *Buckingham Advertiser and Free Press,* 16 January 1892, p.3

7 *Ibid*

8 *Ibid*

9 *Ibid*

10 *Ibid*

11 *Ibid*

12 'Ghosts at Peterborough', *Gloucester Citizen,* 9 January 1892, p.3

13 'Mysterious Manifestations in a Peterborough Cottage', *Buckingham Advertiser and Free Press,* 16 January 1892, p.3

14 *Ibid*

15 'The Peterborough Ghost', *Daily Gazette for Middlesborough,* 23 January 1892, p.3; 'The Ghost Story', *Peterborough Express,* 20 January 1892, p.3

16 'The Ghost Story', *Peterborough Express,* 20 January 1892, p.3

17 'The Peterborough Ghost', *Daily Gazette for Middlesborough,* 23 January 1892, p.3; 'The Ghost Story', *Peterborough Express,* 20 January 1892, p.3

18 'The Alleged Haunted House', *Peterborough Express,* 13 January 1892, p.3

19 'Mysterious Manifestations in a Peterborough Cottage', *Buckingham Advertiser and Free Press,* 16 January 1892, p.3

20 'Interesting Sequel to the Peterborough Ghost', *Peterborough Standard,* 6 February 1892, p.5

21 W. Sydney Robinson, *Muckraker: The Scandalous Life and Times of W.T. Stead* (London: The Rodson Press, 2013)

22 'Interesting Sequel to the Peterborough Ghost', *Peterborough Standard,* 6 February 1892, p.5

23 *Ibid*

24 Robinson (2013), pp.251–254

25 Pardoe Woodman and Estelle Stead, *The Blue Island* (London: Hutchinson and Co, 1922)

Chapter 4: The Christmas Churchyard Riot – The Islington Ghost

1 James Chant, 'A Ghost at St Mary's Churchyard', *Islington Gazette*, 3 January 1899, p.3

2 'The Ghost Trick', *Islington Gazette*, 4 January 1899, p.2

3 'Looking for a Ghost', *Echo*, 1 January 1899, p.2; 'Ghost Scare at Islington', *Globe*, 4 January 1899, p.5; 'Stupid Ghost Hoax', *Bingley Echo*, 4 January 1899, p.8; 'Waiting for a Ghost', *Westminster Gazette*, 4 January 1899, p.5; 'Islington Ghost Scare', *Islington Gazette*, 5 January 1899, p.3

4 'The Hackney Ghost', *Sheffield Evening Telegraph*, 23 August 1895, p.2

5 'Hackney Ghost Hunters', *Morning Leader*, 22 August 1895, p.3; A Hackney Ghost', *Shields Daily Gazette*, 23 August 1895, p.3

6 'The Hackney Ghost Hunt', *London Evening News*, 23 August 1895, p.3; 'The Hackney Ghost', *Sheffield Evening Telegraph*, 23 August 1895, p.2

7 Jacob Middleton, *Spirits of an Industrial Age*, (2014); Owen Davies, *The Haunted: A Social History of Ghosts*, Basingstoke: Palgrave Macmillan, 2007)

8 'Ghost Scare at Islington', *Globe*, 4 January 1899, p.5; 'Islington Ghost Scare', *Islington Gazette*, 5 January 1899, p.3

Chapter 5: Spring-Heeled Jack — The Lochee Ghost

1 For full details see Keith Coleman, *The Cradle, or Dark Lady, of Logie* (2018) available at: http://angusfolklore.blogspot.com/2018/11/the-cradle-or-dark-lady-of-logie.html (accessed: 26 January 2023)

2 Eric Eunson and Bill Early, *Old Dundee* (Stenlake Publishing, 2002)

3 'Preparations for a Donnybrook', *Dundee Evening Post*, 15 December 1900, p.5

4 'Visit of the Spring-heeled Spook to Lochee', *Dundee Evening Telegraph*, 20 December, p5.

5 'Day by Day', *Dundee Evening Post*, 17 December 1900, p.4

6 'Ghost Ridden Dundee', *Dundee Evening Post*, 22 December 1900, p.3

7 'Ghost Appears at Downfield', *Dundee Evening Post*, 17 December 1900, p.6

8 'Ghost Ridden Dundee', *Dundee Evening Post*, 22 December 1900, p.3

9 'More Ghostly Scenes', *Dundee Evening Post*, 25 December 1900, p.4

10 See Jacob Middleton, *Spirits of an Industrial Age* (2018)

11 'Ghosts in Lochee and Broughty Ferry', *Dundee Courier*, 26 December 1900, p.3

12 'Ghosts at Play', *Dundee Evening Post*, 17 December 1900, p.4; 'Lochee's Ghostly Visitant', *Dundee Courier*, 24 December 1900, p.3; 'Ghost Ridden Dundee', *Dundee Evening Post*, 22 December 1900, p.3

13 'Ghost Ridden Dundee', *Dundee Evening Post*, 22 December 1900, p.3

14 'Day by Day,' *Dundee Evening Post*, 21 December 1900, p.4

15 'Ghost Ridden Dundee', *Dundee Evening Post*, 22 December 1900, p.3

16 'Day by Day', *Dundee Evening Post*, 27 December 1900, p.4

17 'Day by day', *Dundee Evening Post*, 26 December 1900, p.4; 'Day by Day', *Dundee Evening Post*, 27 December 1900, p.4

18 'Brutality in Dundee', *Dundee Courier*, 8 September 1902, p.3

19 'A Lochee Ghost Story', *Dundee Evening Post*, 16 September 1902, p.2

Chapter 6: The Violet Farm Poltergeist

1 'The Farmhouse Ghost', *Newcastle Evening Chronicle,* 24 December 1902, p.2; 'The Brierley Ghost', *Sheffield Evening Telegraph,* 3 January 1903; 1901 census

2 'A Christmas Ghost', *Dundee Evening Telegraph,* 24 December 1902, p.3; 'Mr Laybourne's Statement about the Ghost', *Barnsley Chronicle,* 27 December 1902, p.7

3 'A Haunted Farmhouse', *Newcastle Evening Chronicle,* 23 December 1902, p.3; 'Mr Laybourne's Statement about the Ghost', *Barnsley Chronicle,* 27 December 1902, p.7

4 'Mr Laybourne's Statement about the Ghost', *Barnsley Chronicle,* 27 December 1902, p.7

5 'A Haunted Farm', *Dundee Courier,* 26 December 1902, p.5

6 'The Farmhouse Ghost', *Newcastle Evening Chronicle,* 24 December 1902, p.2; 'Mr Laybourne's Statement about the Ghost', *Barnsley Chronicle,* 27 December 1902, p.7

7 'The Farmhouse Ghost', *Newcastle Evening Chronicle,* 24 December 1902, p.2; 'Mr Laybourne's Statement about the Ghost', *Burnsley Chronicle,* 27 December 1902, p.7

8 'The Latest Ghost', *Manchester Courier,* 24 December 1902, p.8

9 'A Haunted Farmhouse', *Newcastle Evening Chronicle,* 23 December 1902

10 'A Haunted Farm', *Dundee Courier,* 26 December 1902, p.5

11 'A Haunted Farmhouse', *Newcastle Evening Chronicle,* 23 December 1902

12 'The Farmhouse Ghost', *Newcastle Evening Chronicle,* 24 December 1902, p.2

13 'The Latest Ghost', *Manchester Courier,* 24 December 1902, p.8

14 'A Ghost Story from Brierley', *Yorkshire Evening Post,* 22 December 1902, p.4; 'A Haunted Farmhouse', *Newcastle Evening Chronicle,* 23 December 1902; A Christmas Ghost', *Dundee Evening Telegraph,* 24 December 1902, p.3

15 'The Brierley Ghost', *Sheffield Evening Telegraph,* 3 January 1903; The Farmhouse Ghost', *Newcastle Evening Chronicle,* 24 December 1902, p.2

16 'A New Sensation', *Barnsley Chronicle,* 10 January 1903, p.7

Chapter 7: The Calverley Ghost – A Yorkshire Tragedy

1 R. V. Holdsworth 'Middleton's Authorship of A Yorkshire Tragedy', *The Review of English Studies,* 45:177 (1994), pp.1–25

2 'Obiter Scripta', *Saint James Gazette,* 22 December 1904, p.4

3 *A Yorkshire Tragedy* Scene ii (6)

4 *A Yorkshire Tragedy* Scene ii (99–102)

5 'Two Unnatural Murders', (1605) republished in T.D. Whittaker, *Loidis and Elmete,*(Leeds, 1816) p.226

6 *A Yorkshire Tragedy* Scene v (105–107)

7 'Two Unnatural Murders' p.228

8 *A Yorkshire Tragedy* Scene viii (18–23)

9 Simon Webb, *Execution: A History of Capital Punishment in Britain* (Stroud: The History Press, 2011) pp.102–106

10 'Tragical Story', *Christian World,* 1 December 1868, p.10

11 *A Yorkshire Tragedy* Scene v (97–98)

12 William Cudworth, *Round About Bradford* (1876) p.452

13 *Annual Register for 1770,* vol 13, p.164

14 *Annual Register for 1770,* vol 13, pp.164–165

15 Edward Garnett, *The Calverley Murders: A Yorkshire Tragedy* (Calverley, 1991) p.40

16 *Ibid* p.33

17 *List of Former Chancellors,* (2023) available at: https://www.cam.ac.uk/about-the-university/how-the-university-and-colleges-work/people/chancellor/former-chancellors (accessed: 27 September 2023)

18 William Cudworth, *Round About Bradford* (1876) p.451; Edward Garnett, *The Calverley Murders: A Yorkshire Tragedy* (Calverley, 1991)

19 1777 according to 'A Christmas Ghost', *Yorkshire Evening Post*, 21 December 1904, p.4.

20 Richard Burdsall, *Memoirs of the Life of Richard Burdsall*, (York, 1797), pp.118–123

21 Garnett, (1991) p.75

22 'Tragical Story', *Christian World*, 1 December 1868, p.10; 'More about the Calverley Ghost', *Yorkshire Evening Post*, 24 December 1904, p.4

23 Garnett (1991) p.76

24 'Calverley Forty Years Ago', *Bradford Observer*, 28 March 1874, p.7

25 *Ibid*

26 John H. Ingram, *The Haunted Homes and Family Traditions of Great Britain* (London: Gibbings and Company, 1897), p.399

27 'A Christmas Ghost', *Yorkshire Evening Post*, 21 December 1904, p.4

28 'A Christmas Ghost', *Cheshire Daily Echo*, 21 December 1904, p.3

29 'More about the Calverley Ghost, *Yorkshire Evening Post*, 24 December 1904, p.4

30 'Alleged Apparition at Horsforth', *Leeds Mercury*, 24 December 1904, p.13

Chapter 8: The Dronfield Skeleton

1 'A Dronfield Ghost Story', *Sheffield Daily Telegraph*, 24 December 1906, p.8

2 'Skeleton Ghost', *Weekly Dispatch*, 30 December 1906, p.3

3 Brian A. Sharpless, 'A Clinician's Guide to Recurrent Isolated Sleep Paralysis', *Neuropsychiatric Disease and Treatment*, 12, (2016) pp.1761–1767 (p.1762)

4 'A Dronfield Ghost Story', *Sheffield Daily Telegraph*, 24 December 1906, p.8

5 David J. Hufford, 'Sleep Paralysis as Spiritual Experience', *Transcultural Psychiatry*, 42 (2005) pp.11–45

6 'Unstone Farm Mystery', *Sheffield Daily Telegraph,* 8 November 1906, p.8; 'Skeleton Found at Unstone', *Derbyshire Times,* 10 November 1906, p.6; 'Unstone Farm Mystery', *Eckington, Woodhouse and Staveley Express,* 10 November 1906, p.5

Chapter 9: The Ghost of King Richard III on New Year's Eve

1 William Shakespeare, *Richard III* Act 5, Scene ii (192–193)

2 Owen Davies, *The Haunted: A Social History of Ghosts* (Basingstoke: Palgrave Macmillan, 2007), p.18

3 Paul Murray Kendall, *Richard III* (London: Sphere Books, 1973), pp.358–369

4 *How Richard III Died,* available at: https://le.ac.uk/richard-iii/identification/osteology/injuries/how-richard-iii-died#:~:text=On%2022%20August%2C%201485%2C%20at,supporters%20who%20cut%20him%20down (accessed: 28 September 2023)

5 A.F. Cross, 'The Ghost of Sutton Ambion', *Nuneaton Chronicle,* 6 January 1922, p.2

6 Leicestershire County Council War Memorial Project, *King Richard's Well, Ambion Field – Sutton Cheney* (2014) available at: http://www.leicestershirewarmemorials.co.uk/war/memorials/view/1109 (accessed: 14 June 2023)

7 A.F. Cross, 'The Ghost of Sutton Ambion', *Nuneaton Chronicle,* 6 January 1922, p.2; 'Bosworth Ghost Scare', *Leicester Evening Mail,* 13 January 1922, p.8

8 A.F. Cross, 'The Ghost of Sutton Ambion', *Nuneaton Chronicle,* 6 January 1922, p.2

9 *Ibid*

10 'Bosworth Ghost Scare', *Leicester Evening Mail,* 13 January 1922, p.8

11 'Bosworth Field Ghost', *Daily News London,* 16 January 1922, p.5

12 *Midland Counties Tribune,* 20 January 1922, p.4

13 The Barn Owl, 'Rambling Richard', *Nuneaton Chronicle,* 21 January 1922, p.3

14 'King Dick Still Walking Abroad', *Nuneaton Chronicle,* 17 March 1922, p.4

15 Jo Appleby et al, 'Perimortem Trauma in King Richard III: a Skeletal Analysis', *Lancet,* 385(9964) pp.253–259, https://doi.org/10.1016/S0140-6736(14)60804-7

16 Tom Evans and Simon Carr, 'King Richard III's 'Ghost' Caught on Camera Peering up from Paving Slabs at Leicester Cathedral', *Daily Mirror,* 21 September 2015. Available at: https://www.mirror.co.uk/news/weird-news/king-richard-iiis-ghost-caught-6489816 (accessed: 28 September 2023)

Chapter 10: The Uxbridge Ghost

1 'Ghost with a Cap', *Daily News,* 7 January 1922, p.1; 'The Uninvited Ghost', *Dundee Courier,* 9 January 1922, p.4; 'White Ghost's Black Bap', *Daily Herald,* 7 January 1922, p.5; The Uxbridge Ghost', *Uxbridge and West Drayton Gazette,* 13 January 1922, p.7

2 'Ghost with a Cap', *Daily News,* 7 January 1922, p.1

3 'The Uxbridge Ghost', *Uxbridge and West Drayton Gazette,* 13 January 1922, p.7

4 'The Uninvited Ghost', *Dundee Courier,* 9 January 1922, p.4

5 Eric Suni and Alex Dimitriu, *Sleep Paralysis: Symptoms, Causes, and Treatment,* (2023) available at: https://www.sleepfoundation.org/parasomnias/sleep-paralysis (accessed: 30 September 2023); Beth Roybal, *Sleep Paralysis* (2023) available at: https://www.webmd.com/sleep-disorders/sleep-paralysis#:~:text=Up%20to%20as%20many%20as,any%20age%20can%20have%20it (accessed: 30 September 2023)

6 'The Uxbridge Ghost', *Uxbridge and West Drayton Gazette,* 13 January 1922, p.7

7 *Ibid*

8 'The Uninvited Ghost', *Dundee Courier*, 9 January 1922, p.4; 'The Uxbridge Ghost', *Uxbridge and West Drayton Gazette*, 13 January 1922, p.7

9 The Uninvited Ghost', *Dundee Courier*, 9 January 1922, p.4; 'The Uxbridge Ghost', *Uxbridge and West Drayton Gazette*, 13 January 1922, p.7; 'Our Ghost', *Uxbridge and West Drayton Gazette*, 20 January 1922, p.7

10 'Uxbridge Ghost Returns', *Uxbridge and West Drayton Gazette*, 27 January 1922, p.12

11 K.C.H. 'The Uxbridge Ghost', *Uxbridge and West Drayton Gazette*, 20 January 1922, p.8

12 Gerald Howson, *The Macaroni Parson: The Life of the Unfortunate Doctor Dodd*, (London: Hutchinson and Co, 1973) p.167

13 *Ibid* p.83

14 *Ibid* p.109

15 *Ibid* p.83

16 *Ibid* p.209

17 *Ibid* pp.222–223

18 See Dodd's entry in the *Newgate Calendar*, available at: https://www.exclassics.com/newgate/ng343.htm

19 K.C.H. 'The Uxbridge Ghost', *Uxbridge and West Drayton Gazette*, 20 January 1922, p.8

20 'Uxbridge Ghost Returns', *Uxbridge and West Drayton Gazette*, 27 January 1922, p.12

Chapter 11: Nurse Matilda – The Asylum Ghost

1 *British Journal of Nursing*, 27 January 1923 vol 51; 'Ghost Asked for Drink', *Reynold's Newspaper*, 14 January 1923, p.9

2 'Ghost Asked for Drink', *Reynold's Newspaper*, 14 January 1923, p.9

3 'Ghost Scare in Ward', *Weekly Dispatch*, 14 January 1923, p.3

4 'Ghost Asked for Drink', *Reynold's Newspaper*, 14 January 1923, p.9

5 *British Journal of Nursing*, 27 January 1923 vol 51

6 'Hospital Ghost', *Shields Daily News*, 14 January 1923, p.4

7 'Ghost Asked for Drink', *Reynold's Newspaper*, 14 January 1923, p.9

8 'Nurse Lays Ghost', *Sunday Post*, 21 January 1923, p.9

9 'Mystery Spook Caught', *Belfast Telegraph*, 22 January 1923, p.3

10 *British Journal of Nursing*, 27 January 1923 vol 51; 'Rochford Ghost', *Chelmsford Chronicle*, 26 January 1923, p.4

11 'The Ghost Walks', *Newcastle Daily Chronicle*, 24 January 1923, p.7

12 'Ghost Sacked', *Liverpool Echo*, 9 July 1926, p.7; 'A Ghost Story', *West Middlesex Gazette*, 17 July 1926, p.5

13 'Mystery Spook Caught', *Belfast Telegraph*, 22 January 1923, p3

14 'Dismissed for a Joke', *Fermanagh Times*, 30 September 1926, p.3

Chapter 12: The Clanking Ghost of East Barnet

1 'The Christmas Ghost', *Belfast Telegraph*, 18 December 1926, p.3; 'Clanking Ghost Again', *Belfast Newsletter*, 23 December 1926, p.10

2 John Horace Round, 'Mandeville, Geoffrey de', *Dictionary of National Biography 1885–1900*, volume 36. Available at: https://en.wikisource.org/wiki/Dictionary_of_National_Biography,_1885-1900/Mandeville,_Geoffrey_de (accessed: 30 September 2023)

3 'Ghosts that Appear at Christmas', *Bournemouth Graphic*, 24 December 1936, p.4

4 'Ghost Changes Quarters', *Daily News*, 22 December 1926, p.8; 'The Barnet Ghost', *Larne Times*, 25 December 1926, p.11

5 'Ghost Changes Quarters', *Daily News*, 22 December 1926, p.8

6 'Christmas Ghost Story', *The Scotsman*, 22 December 1926, p.6

7 'Ghost Changes Quarters', *Daily News,* 22 December 1926, p.8

8 'The Story of a Ghost', *Western Daily Press,* 22 December 1926, p.4

9 'East Barnet Ghost', *Lancashire Evening Post,* 22 December 1926, p.3

10 'The Clankings and Swankings of Geoffrey', *Liverpool Echo,* 23 December 1926, p.4

11 'Clanking Ghost Again', *Belfast Newsletter,* 23 December 1926, p.10

12 'Ghosts that are not Laid', *Daily Herald,* 30 December 1926, p.5

13 'Ghosts of Grey Lady and Earl', *Daily Mirror,* 31 December 1926, p.3; 'A Smiling Ghost', *Belfast Newsletter,* 31 December 1926, p.6

14 'A Smiling Ghost', *Belfast Newsletter,* 31 December 1926, p.6

15 'A Ghost with Dimples', *Gloucester Citizen,* 1 January 1997, p.4

16 *Ibid*

17 'Ghost Hunting in Motor Cars', *Edinburgh Evening News,* 4 January 1927, p.7

18 'Ghosts of Grey Lady and Earl', *Daily Mirror,* 31 December 1926, p.3

19 Ruth Brandon, *The Spiritualists,* (London: Weidenfeld and Nicolson, 1883)

20 'The East Barnet Ghost', *Truth,* 5 January 1928, pp. 26–27

21 'Ghosts of Grey Lady and Earl', *Daily Mirror,* 31 December 1926, p.3

22 'Ghost Maintains its Schedule', *Dundee Evening Telegraph* 28 December 1928, p.4; 'Spook Hunt Fails', *Belfast Telegraph,* 28 December 1928, p.4

23 'A Ghost Drive', *Dundee Evening Telegraph,* 31 December 1928, p.7

24 'Residents in Haunted Neighbourhood Secure £3 Rebate', *Daily Mirror,* 16 January 1929, p.2

25 'Keeping Ghosts to Themselves', *Dundee Evening Telegraph*, 24 December 1929, p.8

26 'Going Ghost Hunting on Christmas Eve: Hysterical Folk Barred', *Belfast Telegraph*, 21 December 1932, p.4

27 'Ghost Arrives on Time', *Weekly Dispatch*, 1 January 1933, p.3

28 'May Scare Ghost', *The People*, 24 December 1933, p.2

29 'This Ghost will be Haunted Tonight', *Daily Mirror*, 24 December 1935, p.4

30 Jack Hallam, *Ghosts of London* (London: Wolf Publishing Company Limited, 1975) p.153

Stocking Fillers: Shorn of the Dead – Shaving Corpses at Christmas

1 'A Singular Christmas Eve Experience', *Gateshead Observer*, 20 December 1879, p.4

2 'Shaving a Dead 'Un', *Yorkshire Gazette*, 24 December 1885, p.11

All images are public domain unless otherwise stated. Every reasonable effort has been made to contact any rights holders.

6TH
BOOKS

ALL THINGS PARANORMAL

Investigations, explanations and deliberations on the paranormal, supernatural, explainable or unexplainable. 6th Books seeks to give answers while nourishing the soul: whether making use of the scientific model or anecdotal and fun, but always beautifully written.

Titles cover everything within parapsychology: how to, lifestyles, alternative medicine, beliefs, myths and theories.

If you have enjoyed this book, why not tell other readers by posting a review on your preferred book site?

Recent bestsellers from 6th Books are:

The Scars of Eden

Paul Wallis

How do we distinguish between our ancestors' ideas of God and close encounters of an extraterrestrial kind?

Paperback: 978-1-78904-852-0 ebook: 978-1-78904-853-7

The Afterlife Unveiled

What the dead are telling us about their world!

Stafford Betty

What happens after we die? Spirits speaking through mediums know, and they want us to know. This book unveils their world...

Paperback: 978-1-84694-496-3 ebook: 978-1-84694-926-5

Harvest: The True Story of Alien Abduction

G.L. Davies

G.L. Davies's most-terrifying investigation yet reveals one woman's terrifying ordeal of alien visitation, nightmarish visions and a prophecy of destruction on a scale never before seen in Pembrokeshire's peaceful history.

Paperback: 978-1-78904-385-3 ebook: 978-1-78904-386-0

Wisdom from the Spirit World

carole j. obley

What can those in spirit teach us about the enduring bond of love, the immense power of forgiveness, discovering our life's purpose and finding peace in a frantic world?

Paperback: 978-1-78904-302-0 ebook: 978-1-78904-303-7

Spirit Release
Sue Allen
A guide to psychic attack, curses, witchcraft, spirit attachment, possession, soul retrieval, haunting, deliverance, exorcism and more, as taught at the College of Psychic Studies.
Paperback: 978-1-84694-033-0 ebook: 978-1-84694-651-6

Advanced Psychic Development
Becky Walsh
Learn how to practise as a professional, contemporary spiritual medium.
Paperback: 978-1-84694-062-0 ebook: 978-1-78099-941-8

Where After
Mariel Forde Clarke
A journey that will compel readers to view life after death in a completely different way.
Paperback: 978-1-78904-617-5 ebook: 978-1-78904-618-2

Poltergeist! A New Investigation into Destructive Haunting
John Fraser
Is the Poltergeist "syndrome" the only type of paranormal phenomena that can really be proven?
Paperback: 978-1-78904-397-6 ebook: 978-1-78904-398-3

A Little Bigfoot: On the Hunt in Sumatra

Pat Spain

Pat Spain lost a layer of skin, pulled leeches off his nether regions, and was violated by an Orangutan for this book.

Paperback: 978-1-78904-605-2 ebook: 978-1-78904-606-9

Astral Projection Made Easy and overcoming the fear of death

Stephanie June Sorrell

From the popular Made Easy series, *Astral Projection Made Easy* helps to eliminate the fear of death through discussion of life beyond the physical body.

Paperback: 978-1-84694-611-0 ebook: 978-1-78099-225-9

Haunted: Horror of Haverfordwest

G.L. Davies

Blissful beginnings for a young couple turn into a nightmare after purchasing their dream home in Wales in 1989.

Paperback: 978-1-78535-843-2 ebook: 978-1-78535-844-9

Readers of ebooks can buy or view any of these bestsellers by clicking on the live link in the title. Most titles are published in paperback and as an ebook. Paperbacks are available in traditional bookshops. Both print and ebook formats are available online.

Find more titles and sign up to our readers' newsletter at **www.6th-books.com**

Join the 6th books Facebook group at **6th Books The world of the Paranormal**

PGIL2024USA